A Consumer's Guide
to
Harmful Investment Products

ANNUITIES • MOST MUTUAL FUNDS

GOLD • WRAP ACCOUNTS • OPTIONS

HEDGE FUNDS • DOZENS OF OTHERS

Earn More. Pay Wall Street Less.

Arthur Paul Ernst

Edited by Robert Pladek

Fiduciary Press LLC

Princeton, NJ

Edited by Robert W. Pladek, Esq.

Published in the United States of America

Fiduciary Press, LLC
P.O. Box 1356
Princeton, NJ 08542

Visit us online at:
www.fiduciarypress.com

First Edition: November 2018

ISBN 978-0-9974185-3-8

Preface

More than any time since the onset of the Great Depression, investors and borrowers are being victimized by the financial industry. Unlike lawyers and doctors, practitioners in finance are not required to act in the best interest of clients. Sadly, there is no industry-wide standard through which you can tell whether an advisor you are speaking with is helping you or steering you for his or her benefit.

There are many ethical advisors who strive to maximize client wealth. Unfortunately, there are far more salespeople who seem similar but instead seek higher fees for themselves and their firms to the financial detriment of their clients.

Several years ago I analyzed some annuities and mutual funds for incoming clients. The principles indicating the benefits of a different course were universal, not specific for these individuals. I expanded these analyses into articles. A number of these articles appeared in various legal journals and a few newspapers. A publisher suggested I write a book if I had enough material to expose at least ten or so rip-offs and schemes. I stopped at about three dozen.

You should not have to depend on happenstance to be properly served. Luckily, you can depend on math and logic. In the pages that follow, in language very accessible to non-financial readers, critical aspects of each product or tactic are exposed so you can clearly understand the potential harm. Easily executed alternative actions are explained. If you still desire to work with a professional, referring to this guide you will be able to distinguish between those who would help you and those who would take advantage of you.

More will be written in the future, but the topics covered in the chapters ahead are those most likely to be impacting you. If you come across an investment product of a dubious or overly costly nature that is not discussed herein, feel free to send a note to the editors at Fiduciary Press, LLC.

Table of Contents

Section I

Introduction

1: Why This Book Was Written

Over the past few decades scandals, bubble bursts, insider deals and huge undeserved bonuses have inspired mistrust of the entire Wall Street community. Changes in law favoring those who bribe and poor net investment returns for the common person only add to this mistrust.

Investors can be classified into one of three groups; those who invest on their own, those who have others invest for them and those who do not invest at all. The fact is you are always investing on your own. If you put money into funds or annuities or hire a professional to pick securities for you, you have decided to invest in that manner and you will profit or lose accordingly. If you avoid stocks and bonds and keep your money in a bank account or pillow case, you've still invested; just poorly. You control your money, and you are responsible for what happens with it.

How can you gainfully handle money while avoiding all that is wrong with Wall Street?

This guide exposes unhelpful, costly and in some cases malicious products so you can overcome the very effective sales tactics Wall Street firms use to separate you from your money. You can easily manage your money well, free of scams and excessive charges. Organized so you can readily find pertinent material, this book also seeks to minimize the time you spend focused on financial matters. You have other things to accomplish and enjoy. Do more of them, with complete confidence your money is appropriately positioned for maximum potential gain.

2: Why Wall Street Fosters So Many Scams

Sutton's Law

Willie Sutton, a prolific bank robber in the 20th century, was famously, if erroneously, credited with a famous quote. Asked by a reporter why he robbed banks, Sutton supposedly answered "because that's where the money is." The message stuck, generating a principle called Sutton's Law which in essence states: when diagnosing a problem, first consider the obvious.

Some people are attracted to the financial industry because of their love of math, appreciation for economics or fascination with commerce. Many more enter the financial field because Wall Street is where the money is. If driven by greed, there is no quicker route to cash than the industry where money is the product. When firms and individuals offer no legitimate expertise or value added, greed can drive them to resort to the worst client-grifting practices.

The psychologies of fear and desire

Financial affairs should be a normal aspect of living, like home maintenance or preparing dinner. Unfortunately, money often becomes an emotional issue. The fear of inadequate resources and a media-fed quest for material acquisition are just two common sources of angst financial companies prey on.

Ads and presentations from sales reps instigate fears that without their services you won't be able to retire, pay for college or survive the next financial crisis. Fear can compel you to pay more for pretty much anything – anything that will take away that fear. Industry pros are trained to take advantage. The extra money they charge worsens your situation, but you feel better about it. You shouldn't.

Big words and bigger egos

Prudent money management is quite easy and the description of the process should be straight forward. Instead, it's often presented in an obtuse fashion replete with highly technical terms. Many professionals will use sophisticated terminology even when describing very simple things to convince clients of their expertise.

If you own a particular stock, bond or fund, you will receive the same dividends and interest and experience the same appreciation as everyone else who owns that security. You do not need to know analyst talking points or the ratios they calculate. In all likelihood, the reps who would talk with you know nothing about them either. But they will cite the words to impress you.

Financial salespeople are famously self-important. If you end up investing or borrowing through them, you are paying for an act, not actual help.

Money is a uniquely uniform product

Most products have distinct attributes. Furniture, clothing and cars vary in style and quality. Prices reflect the supply and demand of particular aspects of each product. This is true of services as well; there are hair stylists, lawyers, plumbers and painters whose talents create choice and price variation.

Money is completely fungible. One dollar is indistinguishable from any other. $1,000 can sit in the bank, a discount brokerage, your wallet or with the classiest boutique money manager in town. It does not matter; it is still worth $1,000.

When you invest, three factors determine your returns: the income from the stocks and bonds you own; their net change in value; and the fees you pay at every level between you and those stocks and bonds. When you borrow, what matters is the cost of borrowing, which factors in all fees and interest and appropriately discounts for time. With both investing and borrowing, your goal should be to maximize your net worth.

Most high-cost and sales-driven financial firms will suggest there are other factors. Commercials hint you will do better with an old company, or a global enterprise, or a franchise with reps who get involved with your personal life. Some institutions emphasize previous performance, while quickly and in small print disclaiming your ability to rely on same. Some firms even promote imprudent behavior, encouraging clients to live beyond their means by taking on excess risk or borrowing at high cost for things they cannot afford. They want you to believe your life will be richer and your money will have more value by dealing with them.

They are wrong. Each dollar will be worth a dollar. You will have more of them if you eliminate sales charges, minimize costs, and avoid scams.

3: What You Will Get Out of This Book

Discover financial rip-offs

Do you own 'B' or 'C' share mutual funds? Are you investing through a 'full-service' broker? Have you ever bought gold, either for gain or as a safe haven? Has anyone tried to sell you an annuity? These costly mistakes and dozens more are identified and explained. You will know to avoid them and learn easy, low cost means to achieve your desired goals.

Know who you can trust

Financial products are sold by anyone who can score 70% on a relatively easy test to gain a license. Advisors who sell annuities and loaded mutual funds in particular are likely to be math-challenged salespeople from other lines of work who crossed into finance for better commissions. You will see why they should not be trusted and learn which institutions and professionals are most helpful.

Manage money well with minimal effort

Unlike academic tomes, misleading "get rich quick" schemes or historical narratives often deducing false lessons, this book concisely outlines the cogent steps you can follow to easily construct a risk-appropriate, cost-efficient portfolio. You will know how to minimize costs and eliminate unhelpful interference.

In sum, you will quickly be able to get on with the rest of your life protected from scammers and confident your financial accounts are working maximally for your benefit.

4: You Invest and Borrow on Your Own

In medicine, doctors must abide by the Hippocratic Oath, often summed up by a phrase from The History of Epidemics: "first, do no harm." In law, the rules of professional responsibility require lawyers to act in the interest of their clients.

In finance, most professionals operate without such a code. Consider the classic broker-dealer as an operating unit. Dealers make money buying assets at a certain price and selling them at a higher price. Brokers make money generating transactions. By its very construct, a broker-dealer makes money at the expense of its clients.

Financial representatives, whatever their title (broker, consultant, planner, counselor, etc.) represent their firms and themselves, not you. Unlike the doctor and lawyer, a financial rep can legally act against your interest. He can charge you exorbitant fees, sell you unsafe securities, and build an imprudent portfolio as long as he provides required disclosures. The positive aspects of products are loudly spoken and advertised. The risks, fees, and damaging aspects are written in tiny letters toward the back of lengthy, rarely read documents.

With or without a professional, it is your money which is at risk. You are the investor. The responsibility is never truly borne by others. You are on your own.

5: How This Book Is Organized

Section II

Chapters 6 to 34 highlight investment products you should avoid. Some are imprudent. Many are ineffective. Most are overpriced, charging fees without adding value.

Section III

Chapters 35 to 42 discuss widely used strategies more harmful than helpful. Some are vigorously pushed because they had recent, fleeting success or are merely easy to explain. These are not legitimate portfolio practices. They are stylish antics with easily recited catch phrases suckering in the unwary or uninformed.

Section IV

Chapters 43 to 50 show a simple investment regimen which, analytically with historical support, should maximize your expected returns with a level of risk appropriate to your tolerance.

Section V

Chapters Finally, appendices are included for quick reference to gainful securities, excellent low-cost institutions, and information frequently cited in the book.

.

Section II

Investment Vehicles You Should Avoid

6: Why You Need to Invest in Stocks and Bonds

With market dips, frauds, trading scandals, and the products exposed herein, you may be tempted to avoid stocks and bonds entirely. If all of your money was in an extremely secure place such as a bank account or money market fund, you could ignore the news. You would have no regrets on those occasions when the market crashes or fraud is uncovered.

Though money sitting in a bank account is not exposed to movements in equity and fixed income markets, it is exposed to the world – a world of inflation and economic activity. Such money is still invested; it rests in a vehicle not rising with economic growth as stocks do; one yielding far less than bonds; a vehicle falling in real value as prices on the things you buy rise.

The fact cash doesn't 'go down' might provide comfort to the ultra-conservative or inert. Don't let it. The value of money is its power to purchase things. If the prices of the things you want double over the course of a time when your assets don't change in value, your purchasing power will have dropped by half.

Figure 6-1: Growth of $10,000 1968 - 2017

—— Stocks – – Bonds ‑‑‑ Cash

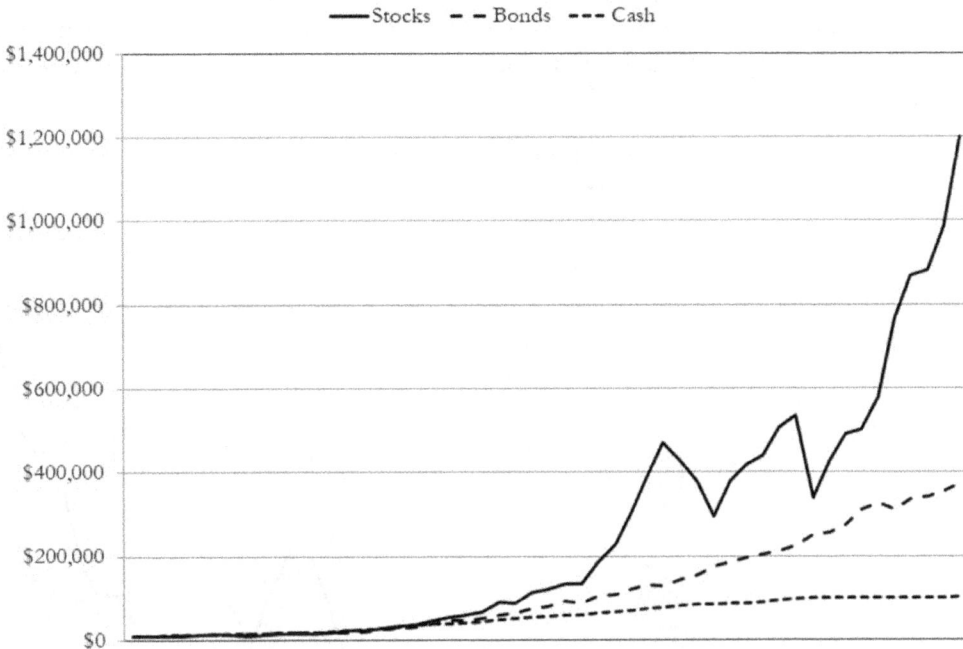

In Figures 6-1 and 6-2 you can see how $10,000 grew over time if invested in stocks, bonds and cash equivalents (bank accounts, money market funds, Treasury bills).

Figure 6-2: Growth of $10,000 2008 - 2017

———Stocks – – Bonds - - - Cash

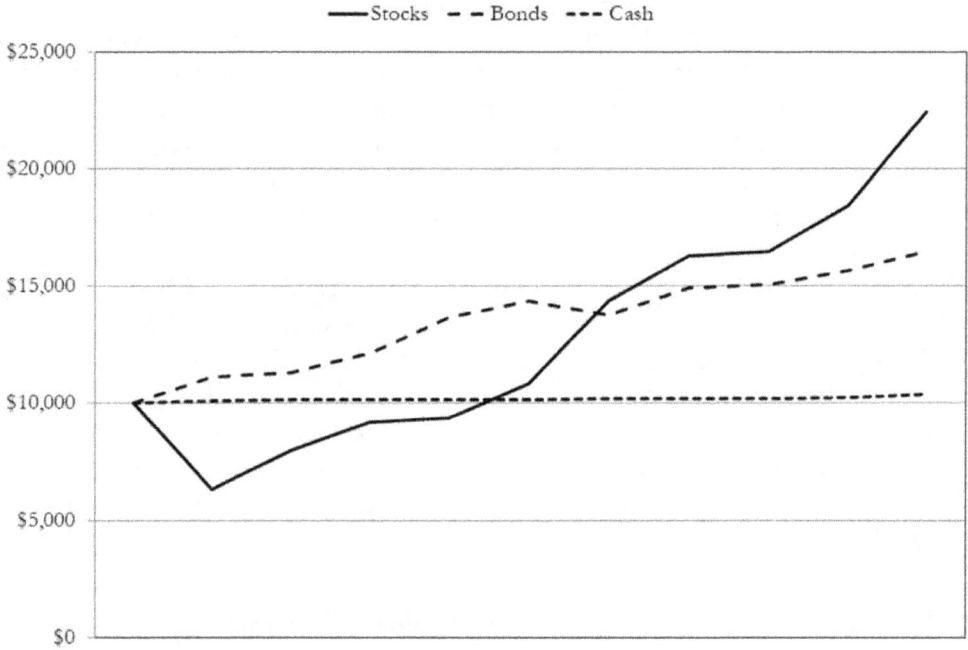

In Figures 6-3 and 6-4 you see how $10,000 would have grown in real terms – meaning adjusted for inflation – if invested in stocks, bonds and cash.

Figure 6-3: Inflation Adjusted Growth 1968 - 2017

———Stocks – – Bonds - - - Cash

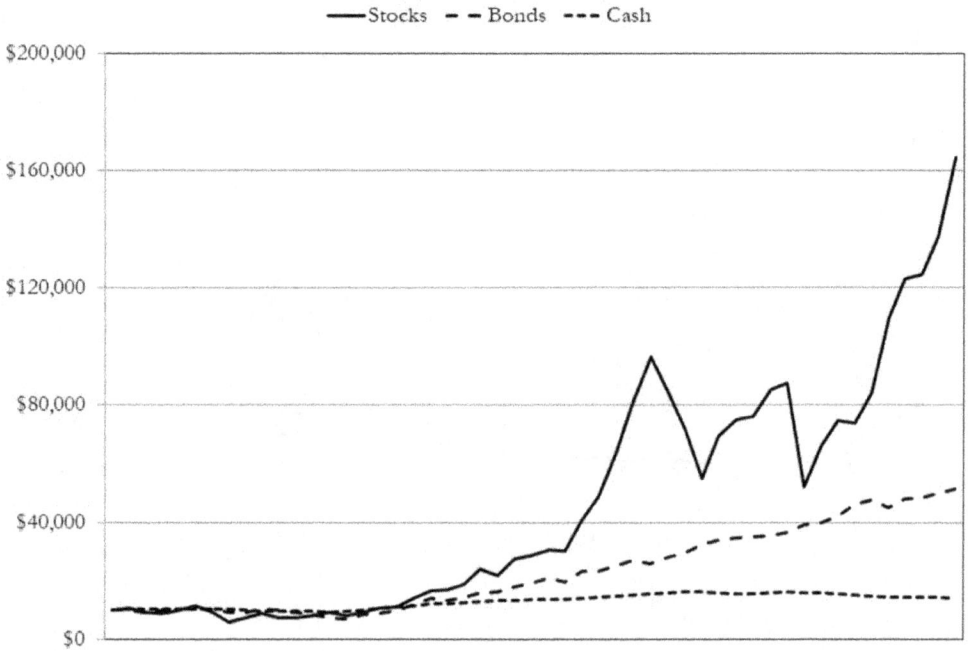

Two things stand out in these charts. First, inflation is impactful. Over the 50 years 1968 through 2017, $10,000 invested in stocks grew to almost $1.2 million. In terms of real purchasing power, over the same period that same $10,000 stock portfolio only grew to about $160,000.

Figure 6-4: Inflation Adjusted Growth 2008 - 2017

—— Stocks — — Bonds - - - Cash

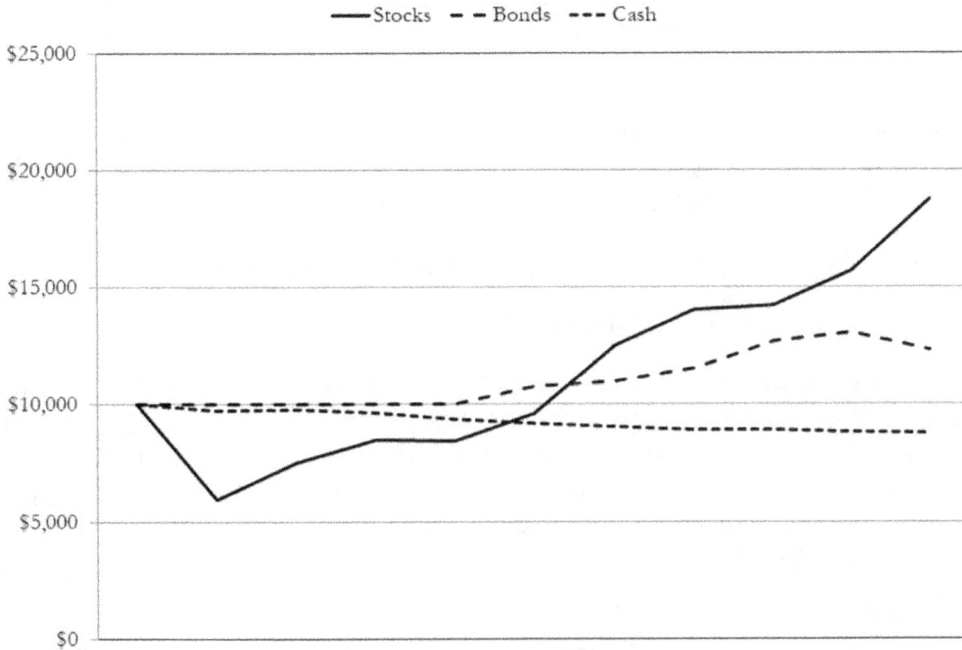

Second, inflation can outpace cash over long spells. From 2008 through 2017, an all Treasury bill portfolio grew from $10,000 to about $10,408; adjusted for inflation it shrunk to less than $8,800.

The goal of investing is to grow the value – the real, inflation adjusted worth – of your assets. As the charts make clear, cash provides the least effective and stocks the most effective means of growing wealth and beating inflation. It is also clear stocks are volatile while bonds and cash lend stability to a portfolio. So it's wise to hold some of each asset category. Determining the breakdown right for you is an important topic covered in Chapters 45 and 46.

* Data sources:
Stock returns: S&P Dow Jones Indices LLC; Standard & Poor's 500 Index.
Bond returns: Federal Reserve Release H-15; An index of equal parts (25% each) Moody's Aaa corporate bonds, Moody's Baa corporate bonds, 5-year Treasury bonds, and 10-year Treasury bonds, rebalanced annually.
Inflation: U.S. Department of Labor, Bureau of Labor Statistics; Consumer Price Index.

7: Alternative Securities

What is an alternative investment?

"Alternatives" are investments that are not stocks, bonds, cash instruments, or funds made up of those things. Common ones include gold (Chapter 38) and other commodities (Chapter 11), options (Chapter 32) and other derivatives (Chapter 12), hedge funds (Chapter 15) and real estate (Chapter 34)

The chief attribute sought in an alternative investment is behavior – price movement – that differs from the regular markets. For example, if you think the stock market is going down, you would like to own something going in the opposite direction. That's the theory.

Why you should avoid alternative investments

Different is not better

One fundamental problem with alternatives is that regular markets generally go up. Despite occasional down drafts and rare panics, over time wealth is increased by owning stocks and bonds. If the defining characteristic of a particular asset is opposite movement to the market, why put money into something expected to go down? Indeed, options lose their premiums over time, certain commodities have declined over long spells and poorly located real estate has damaged many portfolios.

Gambling is not investing

You have probably seen headlines about massive profits earned in alternative investments. Gold was hot in 1979 and in the years surrounding the financial collapse of 2008. Real estate had a broad boom in the 1980s and upward spurts in various locations as local economic conditions allowed. Certain hedge fund managers gained fame when their firms recorded incredible gains. However, you probably did not see articles highlighting gold's 21 year drop after 1980 and its fall since 2011. Nor have you seen much about real estate investing since the 2008 financial debacle made a mockery of house flipping and other short-sighted tactics. And those hot hedge fund managers? Turns out their long-term returns are worse than basic index funds and some of their boasted gains not a product of genius, but illegal insider tips.

Basically, anything can go up in value and look like an investment. But that upward movement does not make it one. Alternative investments are speculative vehicles. Committing money to this sector instead of stocks and bonds is a gamble – actually two gambles. First, by taking money out of the market you gamble on stocks and bonds not generating returns for a spell. This is market timing, a technique demonstrably harmful to investors (Chapter 42). Second, you are gambling on the alternative security. It may go up. It may not. Over time, it will most likely go up far less than the stocks and bonds you gambled against, as experience has shown.

What you should do instead

If your interest in alternative investments is anticipated pie-in-the-sky returns, come back to earth and seek the solid gains obtainable in the stock and bond markets. Avoid the tempting thought you know more about gold, land or derivatives than the professionals whose opinions are already reflected in current prices. And resist the claims of salespeople pushing alternative products and hedge funds; bad holdings coupled with huge fees is a recipe for disaster.

If your interest in alternatives arises from extreme market fears and a desire for capital preservation, your tolerance for risk may have shifted. Consider selling some of your stocks or stock funds and either hold the cash generated or buy some short-term bonds or CDs. Once your fear subsides and your risk tolerance shifts back in the other direction, return to your longer-term, risk appropriate asset allocation.

8: Annuities

What is an annuity?

An annuity is a contract through which you pay money now to receive a stream of income in the future. While some begin payments shortly after the contract is signed and paid for, most pay only after much time has passed.

There are many types of annuities, all of which entail the negative aspects outlined below. For simplicity and space, the description here focuses on the most heavily promoted product, the variable annuity.

A variable annuity is presented as an investment platform with an array of fund choices. The time gap between paying your premium and later receiving your income is called the 'accumulation period' during which the value of the funds within the annuity theoretically grows. When you decide to start receiving payments, the accumulation period ends. On that day, the day of annuitization, the accumulation value is tallied by combining all assets. This accumulation value is multiplied by a factor to determine how much money the annuity will pay you going forward.

Some annuities offer the ability to lock in a fixed dollar amount of income. Others offer minimum amounts of income which could be exceeded if your funds perform better than expected. Many are sold with minimum growth rates of your accumulation value whereby two balances are tracked: your actual investment balance, and a phantom balance that benefits from the minimum growth rate.

Annuities are not bad, conceptually. Arranging for an assured flow of funds streaming in for a given period, perhaps even for the rest of one's life, is tempting. The problems with annuities relate to their execution.

Why you should avoid Annuities

Sales commissions

One reason annuities are hawked so hard is the huge sales commission, often in the area of 5-10% of the amount invested. If you buy a $100,000 annuity, $5,000 or more of your money can go directly to the rep.

High fees

Administrative costs charged to annuities are notorious, often 2-3% of assets annually. No matter what investments are held in the underlying account, reducing returns by that much each year will crush long-term performance.

Misleading growth guarantees

To counter concerns over high fees and market uncertainties, many annuities are sold with a guaranteed minimum growth rate. However, this minimum growth rate pertains to a nominal accumulating value, the "phantom" balance referred to above. If you want to pull your money out, you only have access to your actual, fee-damaged, market impacted account value. The guaranteed amount is just a number that might be used for calculating payments upon annuitization.

Misleading income guarantees

Following the previous point, you might think the guaranteed growth feature works well as long as you do not pull out early. Unfortunately, the amount of income you receive depends on two figures: the accumulation value and a factor. This factor comes from a table in the annuity contract. A typical table might indicate that for every $1,000 of accumulated value, you could choose to receive $4 per month for life, or $3.50 per month for life with 20 years of payments guaranteed, or some other combination of amount and guaranty. To the point, when annuities offer a guaranteed accumulation growth rate, they usually provide two factor tables. The table used with the guaranteed value will have factors far lower than those in the table used with the actual investment value. After applying these factors, one can estimate real rates of return based solely on cash invested and cash received. As of this writing, annuities advertising guaranteed accumulation growth of 6-7% actually provide returns in the 2-3.5% range. The levels in the guaranty quotes are shams.

Penalties for changing your mind

Exiting an annuity is not cheap. For the first several years after purchase, you will have to pay a surrender charge to get your money back. Penalties often start in the 5-8% range and decline annually until they vanish. The surrender charge provides the seller enough of your money to pay all sales commissions and still leave a healthy profit.

Poor performance

Administrative fees alone impede performance to the point where the underlying portfolios in annuities are destined to do poorly. Additionally, since the underlying funds used in many annuities do not compete directly for assets, fund management is often lackluster.

Figure 8-1: Annuity vs Regular Investment Account

······ Annuity Cash Flow	- - - Investment Account Cash Flow
—— Annuity Balance Available	– – Investment Account Balance Available

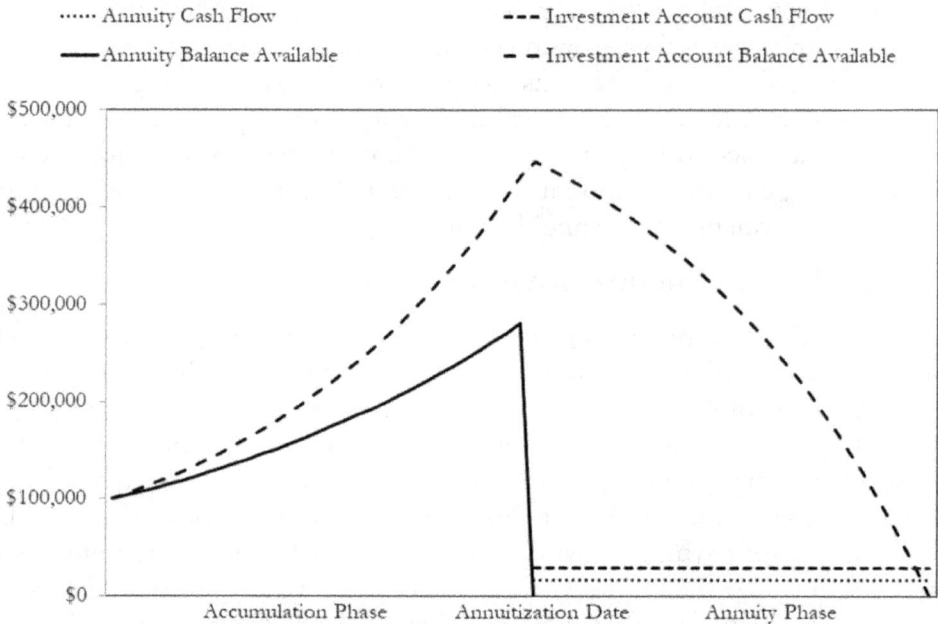

Lack of control

When you have money in a bank or brokerage account, you can access it at any time. After you purchase an annuity, you have hurdles. Early withdrawal/surrender penalties mean you will not be able to get all of your money back during the first few years. Once the surrender charges finally cease, the amount returned to you will have been depleted from excessive fees paid over all those years. Finally, after the annuity switches from the accumulation phase to the paying annuity phase, you have no access at all to any money beyond the payment stream.

Figure 8-1 demonstrates the net effect of an annuity's harmful features. Two choices are modeled; an investment account that earns 5% annually and an annuity entailing 1.5% fees (well below average) whose underlying investments also earn 5% annually. After 30 years of accumulation (growth), both choices start paying cash; the annuity using a factor of 6% of the account value on the annuitization date, and the investment account at a pace that leaves nothing at the end of 30 years.

Briefly, lower fees with the same investments allow the investment account to generate 80% more cash flow than the annuity. Given a beginning balance of $100,000, the investment account described provides a 30-year stream of $29,520 per year; the annuity just $16,841 per year. As important, during the life of the investment account, the owner has access to the entire balance. With the annuity, during the accumulation phase the owner has access to a penalty reduced amount in the initial years, fee damaged amounts until annuitization and only the payment stream thereafter.

What you should do instead

If you are considering annuities as a one-stop solution to your investing needs, execute a proper investment regimen instead. Refer to Section IV for an easy-to-execute plan.

If you are considering annuities as a source of steady cash flow, seek sources of income that avoid all those negatives associated with annuities. Bonds and high dividend stocks or stock funds could make sense. When evaluating these investments, do not be discouraged by yields that seem lower than advertised annuity rates. Annuity yields are not comparable to other yields. With annuities you never get your principal back.

Finally, if you are considering annuities as a retirement / end of life vehicle, know that the annuity dies when you die. There are optional terms you can add to guarantee a certain number of payments should you die soon after payments start, but the cost of these options reduces the rate of return from bad to pathetic.

* Data sources:
The "Regular Investment Account" assumes a deposit of $100,000, 5% annual growth for 30 years, and constant withdrawals calculated to eliminate the balance in 30 years. Given the assumptions, monthly payments are $2,460.05. Over 30 years they add up to $885,618.
The annuity assumes a $100,000 purchase with underlying funds earning 5% annually and a 1.5% expense rate. The balance available assumes an early withdrawal penalty of 8%. Cash flow assumes a "factor" of six. Given the assumptions, monthly payments are $1,684.08. Over 30 years they add up to $606,267.

9: Art

What is art?

As an investment, art is simply an object with perceived value. If the perception improves, the value will rise. Increased interest in the artist or style can help. Supply and demand factors are also important, especially if an artist is no longer alive. Impediments include new artwork as well as the mass production of absolutely anything that can be displayed.

Every now and then we read about famous paintings auctioned off for fortunes. Many of the reports highlight record breaking prices for the given artist, style, or era. With records continually set, one can easily associate increasing art values with price behavior analogous to stocks and bonds. Art also looks great, or at least it should in the eyes of its owner.

Why you should avoid art as an investment

Maintenance

If you buy art with the intention of selling it for profit, you will have to keep it in proper condition. Most paintings, sculptures and artifacts must be kept in highly controlled environments, with strict and quite narrow ranges for temperature and humidity. Protection from theft and fire are also vital. The cost of all this maintenance diminishes potential gains. Failure in any one area of maintenance will wipe out your investment altogether.

Liquidity

You should be able to easily convert your investments into cash at known values. Stocks, bonds, and funds trade every day; you can calculate the exact amount of cash you would receive upon sale at any time. Art, however, changes hands at infrequent auctions and even less competitive private offerings. The works brought for sale at such venues are only worth the amount a buyer on hand is willing to pay. That amount may be a lot, or not. It is certainly not known. If the artist whose work you ponied up a small fortune for is not in demand, you may be looking at garage sale prices.

Competitive disadvantage

If you are an expert in art, not just knowledgeable about its history but rather fully aware of the auction process and the various supply and demand factors affecting prices, you can probably ignore this chapter. If you are not an expert, be aware that there are indeed experts out there whose main source of profit is taking advantage of people like you.

What you should do instead

Simply put, decorate your house in whatever manner you want it to look. Maintain your home environment at whatever temperatures and humidity levels make you most comfortable. Lastly, keep your investment dollars directed toward securities in a logical, liquid fashion. Section IV can be read and grasped in less time than a single art auction.

10: Brokerage Wrap Accounts

What is a brokerage wrap account?

In a standard brokerage account, fees are generated every time there is a transaction. Brokers with clients in such accounts have the incentive to come up with reasons to trade. Notorious practitioners often churn client accounts, buying and selling frequently to beef up their own income at the expense of their clients. When caught, these brokers and their firms are punished. In an attempt to maintain fee income and remove the incentive to trade, the wrap account was created.

Wrap accounts charge owners a set fee, usually 1% to 3% of assets, with an annual minimum, perhaps $1,000 to $3,000. For this fee, the client can trade as often or infrequently as desired. Usually there are a maximum number of included trades, with marginal trading fees added when that maximum is exceeded. Often other services, like sending wires, checking, and such are free or otherwise covered within the 'wrap'.

Why you should avoid brokerage wrap accounts

Damaging sales fees

Wrap fees do not pay for money management. Wrap fees are sales commissions. Their damaging magnitude assumes fairly active trading at the highest possible cost. Wrap fees wipe out much, perhaps all, of the income you might receive from dividends and bond interest. Based on historical returns, wrap fees can inhibit stock growth by 20-30% or more.

Figure 10-1 exhibits the reduction to returns on stocks, bonds, and a balanced portfolio of each for the decade 2008-2017. Figure 10-2 shows the impact on dollar growth for the two decades ending 2017. Invested in a 50/50 allocation between stocks matching returns on the Standard & Poor's 500 and bonds performing apace a blend of high grade bonds*, $10,000 would have grown to over $39,000 from 1998 to 2017. Invested in the exact same manner in a wrap account with a 1.5% fee, the ending balance would instead have been about $29,000; a $10,000 hit on a $10,000 investment.

Lack of service

When an account generates commissions on each transaction, there is incentive for a broker to come up with reasons to trade, whether the ideas are well-intentioned or not. With a wrap account, wherein fees are earned regardless of activity, there is little incentive for a broker to come up with any ideas. In fact, the goal of most client facing brokers is to gather assets for their firm and put those assets into accounts that generate continuous fees.

These charges will grow regardless of service, allowing the brokers to move on to gather more assets. Wrap accounts commonly get little attention.

Figure 10-1: Wrap Effect on Returns 2008-2017

⬛ No Wrap   ⊟ With Wrap

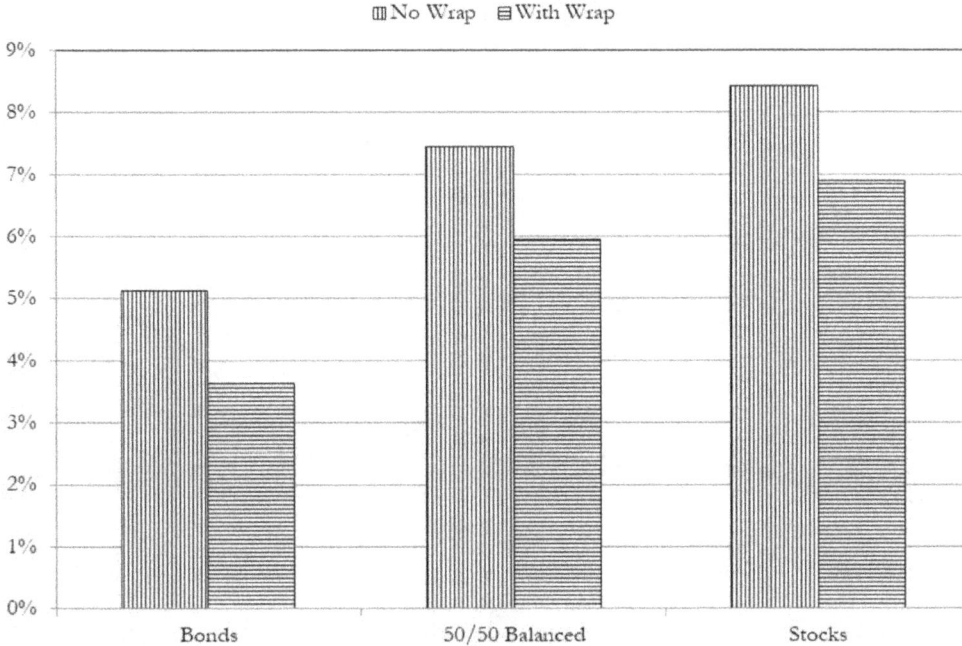

Double charges for management

The wrap fee you pay merely compensates salespeople. If you want actual asset management, your money will either be placed into mutual funds or into a consulting arrangement whereby a third party will manage your portfolio. In both cases, management fees will be charged, all supplemental to the already-harmful wrap fees.

Marginal legality

In 2007, the U.S. Court of Appeals for the D.C. Circuit deemed wrap accounts based solely on annuitized commissions to be illegal. The court held that the firms charging these fees must be held to fiduciary standards consistent with the Investment Company Act of 1940. In response, the major brokerages created "comprehensive" wrap accounts through which advice would be provided to fee paying clients. Unfortunately, these firms did not send their salespeople to graduate business programs or other institutions where they might have learned something about portfolio management. The new brochures became wordier, the reports more graphically intense and the jargon laced with impressive terms. But the wrap accounts are essentially the same, and the "advisors" and "consultants" proffering them are still salespeople.

Figure 10-2: Wrap Effect on Dollar Growth 1998-2017

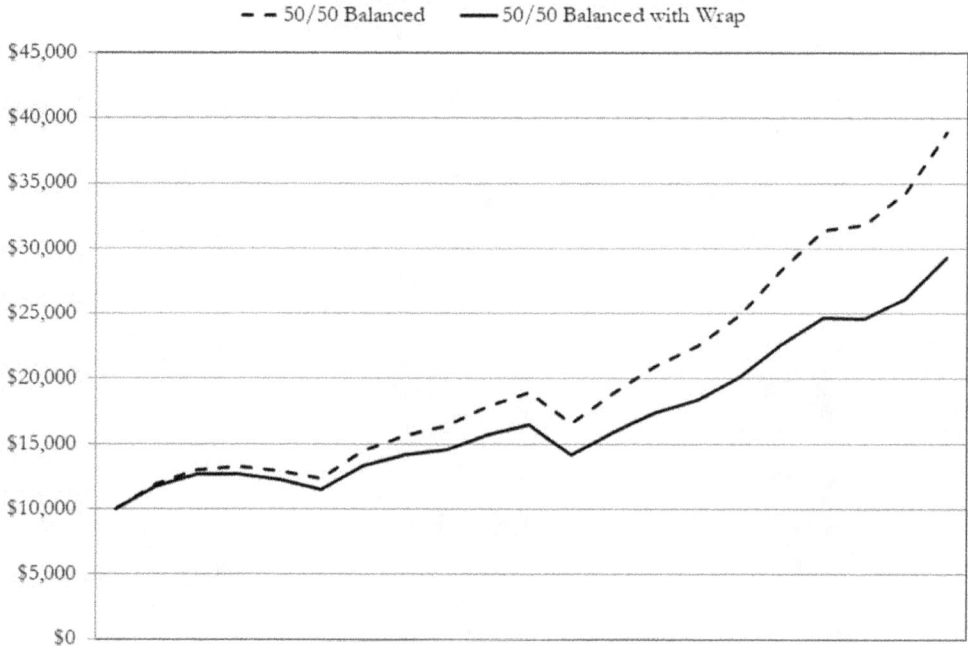

- - 50/50 Balanced ——— 50/50 Balanced with Wrap

What you should do instead

Plain and simple, do not open a wrap account. If your money is in a wrap account, get it out. Open an account at a discount broker such as Schwab or TD Ameritrade or Vanguard (Appendix A) and transfer your assets. If you want active management by a devoted portfolio manager, seek a good and fiduciary registered investment advisor (Chapter 50).

* Data sources:
Stock returns: S&P Dow Jones Indices LLC; Standard & Poor's 500 Index.
Bond returns: Federal Reserve Release H-15; An index of equal parts (25% each) Moody's Aaa corporate bonds, Moody's Baa corporate bonds, 5-year Treasury bonds, and 10-year Treasury bonds, rebalanced annually.
Balanced returns assume 50% each stock and bonds, rebalanced annually.
Wrap fee: 1.5%

11: Commodities

What is a commodity?

Briefly put, a commodity is stuff. More precisely, it is a contract for the future delivery of stuff. Rarely do investors take delivery of cattle or piles of wheat. Contract prices move up and down according to market conditions, and at some point before the delivery date an offsetting transaction should occur. If you had purchased something, you sell it; and if you had sold it, you would need to buy it. Regardless of the order in which you bought and sold, your profit would be the difference between selling and buying prices. Meanwhile no actual commodities change hands.

Commodities have a purpose beyond speculation or theoretical investment. Farmers can guarantee a certain level of income by agreeing to sell their product at an opportune time instead of depending on prices at harvest. Food manufacturers can lock in costs and supplies buying from these farmers ahead of time. Similar activities allow miners, oil drillers, and other extractors to secure income levels while simultaneously allowing utilities, manufacturers and processors to lock in costs and needed inputs.

For the rest of us, who neither produce nor use raw materials, commodities are just another way to make or lose money. Examples of what investors can bet on include precious metals such as gold, silver and platinum; industrial metals such as steel and copper; and agricultural products such as wheat, corn, cattle and the classic pork bellies.

Why you should avoid investing in commodities

No expectation of return

Commodities entail no earnings, no income, no operations – no innate reason for growth. Though it is logical to expect commodities to keep pace with inflation, the growing service orientation of our economy combined with productivity gains has frequently led to spells in which commodities drop in value despite price increases in other areas.

It is a gamble you will probably lose

Commodities represent a bet – pure speculation. Buying and selling in these markets, for a non-producer or user, is like playing blackjack or craps in Las Vegas. You might win. But you probably won't.

Do you have a better read on weather and harvests than farmers and agricultural experts? Do you understand metals better than geologists and mining experts? Did you attend the most recent OPEC meeting? If you answer 'no' to all three questions, you are at a terrible disadvantage, playing with a stacked deck where the other players know the card order.

What you should do instead

If your interest in commodities stems from reduced confidence in the regular securities markets, you would be better served by adjusting your asset allocation to a more conservative stance. You might sell some stock holdings and keep a higher portion of your assets in cash or bonds for a spell. Market timing should be avoided (Chapter 42), but if your tolerance for risk is seriously reduced, taking corrective action is not wrong.

If you fear inflation and think commodities might provide some protection, remember stocks have historically provided the best hedge against rising prices. Thanks to the hard work of employees, guidance of managers and ownership of real property, corporate stock values tend to appreciate at a higher rate than consumer prices. Instead of gambling with commodities, beat inflation with time-proven equities.

Figure 11-1: Inflation vs Oil, Gold, Stocks 1983-2017

– – Oil   ······· Gold   - - - Stocks   —— Price Index

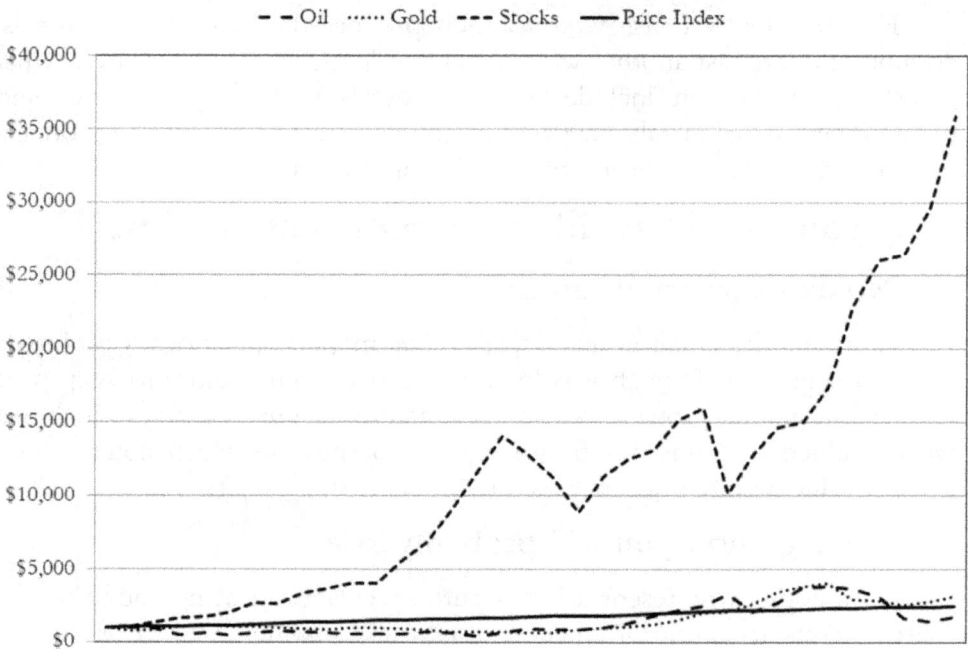

If you're thinking of commodities as a way to make a lot of money by outguessing experts, be realistic. Only put to risk an amount that you would take, and fully expect to lose, on a trip to Las Vegas or Atlantic City. Better yet, don't put anything at risk.

* Data sources:
Stock returns: S&P Dow Jones Indices LLC; Standard & Poor's 500 Index.
Oil prices: BP Statistical Review of World Energy, Brent crude.
Gold prices: COMEX – Commodity Exchange Inc., New York Mercantile exchange since 1994.
Price index: U.S. Department of Labor, Bureau of Labor Statistics, Consumer Price Index

12: Derivatives

What is a derivative?

Derivative is a catchall term for an instrument that is not like a stock or bond itself but rather a contract with rights to purchase or sell something of value at some point in the future. Some derivatives obligate both the buyer and seller to execute the future transaction. Others grant the option to transact to the buyer of the contract. There are many types of derivatives, but the two main ones are futures (Chapter 14) and options (Chapter 32). The comments below are pertinent to derivatives in general.

Why you should avoid derivatives

They are not investments

It is possible and sometimes probable you could buy a derivative and never exercise the rights therein, forfeiting every penny spent. Conversely, if you sell a certain derivative to augment income, you could end up owing many times more money than you received. Something rendering no actual material ownership with the reasonable likelihood of losing all of your money (or more) is not an investment. It is irresponsible speculation.

Competitive disadvantage

Unlike stocks, where all investors can gain as a growing economy fosters rising markets, most derivatives are zero-sum games. One person's gain is another's loss. In the days and months after the derivative transaction, price movements of the underlying security or commodity will hurt one contract party as much as it helps the other. In each market, there are interested experts who specialize in the analysis and trading of both derivatives and the underlying items. In a zero-sum game, your chances of out trading devoted professionals are almost nil.

What you should do instead

If your interest in buying a derivative is based on a favorable view of its underlying security, ignore the derivative and buy the underlying security directly. Potential returns may not be as dramatic, but potential losses won't be, either. Further, derivatives expire, and it is possible your favorable opinion will be proven right – but only after the derivative's expiration date. If you bought the item directly you could still profit; with the derivative, you would have lost all.

If your interest in selling a derivative is to increase income, find such income elsewhere – or do without. If you need more income there are safer means, such as high dividend paying stocks or more aggressive bond positions. These have risks too, but nothing approaching the devastation derivatives can bring. Good investing means seeking upside potential and limiting downside risk. Derivatives bring the opposite.

13: ETFs Not Indexed to Stocks

What is an exchange traded fund?

Similar to mutual funds (Chapter 18), exchange traded funds (ETFs) are companies through which assets of shareholders are pooled to achieve pro-rata ownership of a diversified portfolio. Usually an ETF will seek to replicate the performance of a particular part of the market. For instance, one can find ETFs that mimic the Standard & Poor's 500, an index of Chilean stocks, long-term government bonds and so forth.

In general, ETFs provide an excellent avenue through which you can obtain a diversified portfolio. Most have very low costs and present well-structured index exposures. Examples of these ETFs are listed in Appendix B and discussed in Section IV.

Of course, Wall Street could not leave well enough alone. Seeing the growing popularity of investor-friendly ETFs, less investor-friendly ones have sprouted up to suck in more revenue. Some new funds are index vehicles with a benign mission but needlessly high expenses. Many new ETFs have esoteric goals aimed to take advantage of investor fear and greed. Some promise to move in the opposite direction of a particular market. Others profess to rise or fall by a multiple of a specific index. Combined with ETFs that provide exposure to commodities, real estate and currencies, a whole new universe of alternatives has been created.

Why you should avoid non-index, non-equity ETFs

Bad contents make bad funds

ETFs consist of the securities purchased and held within the fund. If the fund invests in vehicles you would not buy directly, you should not invest in the fund. As explained in other chapters, you should not buy ETFs that invest in commodities (Chapter 11), currencies (Chapter 22), futures (Chapter 14) and options (Chapter 32). Also, since you should not try to time the market (Chapter 42), stay away from bear market ETFs and anything promising to go up when the market goes down (Chapter 20). Further, since professional mutual fund managers have underperformed indexes over time (Chapter 29), avoid managed, non-index ETFs as well. Similarly, per arguments highlighting bad attributes of their mutual fund equivalents, you should also keep clear of ETFs based on asset allocation (Chapter 19), bonds (Chapter 21), long/short positions (Chapter 28) and target dates (Chapter 30).

You should avoid risk, not magnify it

A number of ETFs sell the prospect of moving multiple times the rate of change of a given index. If the Standard & Poor's 500 goes up 2%, an ETF designed to double the index's pace should rise 4%. When that happens, holders are happy. But when the market declines, a holder will drop at twice the magnitude...and more.

To create this multiplier effect, these ETFs buy and sell derivatives (Chapter 12). These bring on transaction costs, risk, and in the case of options a continual drain of premium. On any given day these ETFs may meet their goals of multiplying returns. Over time, most will drift downward to levels well below the value pure multiplication would indicate.

Figure 13-1: Degradation of an Inverse ETF 12/2006 - 3/2011

A good example of this phenomenon is the experience of ticker symbol SDS, the ProShares UltraShort S&P500 ETF. This fund is designed to move in the opposite direction of, and by twice as much as, the change in the S&P 500 Index. Figure 13-1 plots the value of $10,000 invested in SDS from the end of 2006 through March of 2011 – a period that begins and ends with the S&P 500 at the same level. Also shown is the course of $10,000 invested in ticker SPY, the SPDR S&P 500 ETF. This ETF is designed to move in the same direction and at the same pace as the S&P 500 Index. Given the stated goals, one would expect values of these single security portfolios to mirror each other, with SDS moving opposite of, and with twice the magnitude as, SPY.

In reality, SDS performed far worse than expected. In September 2009, when the S&P portfolio was still about 25% below the 2007 starting level, SDS should have been 50% higher. Instead, it had fallen back to its original level. When the S&P portfolio recovered enough to reach its original $10,000 in February 2011, the SDS portfolio should have also been about $10,000; instead it was below $5,000.

Adding risk and reducing returns is the opposite of good investing.

What you should do instead

As part of a proper investment regimen, absolutely consider low-cost index exchange traded funds that invest directly in stocks, without leverage or derivatives. Chapter 48 and Appendix B provide guidance for fund selection.

If you are considering bond ETFs, read Chapter 49 to improve your approach.

Avoid all other ETFs.

* Data source:
New York Stock Exchange: Closing prices for tickers SPY and SDS.

14: Futures

What is a future?

A futures contract, often abbreviated as 'future', represents the purchase or sale of something with a future settlement date. When you buy a future, you own the item with all the opportunity for gain and risk of loss. But the item is not yet delivered, and beyond the transaction cost of the contract, cash does not change hands.

Futures have three key attributes: (1) the underlying thing, such as a commodity or currency; (2) the price at which this thing is bought or sold, called the settlement price; and (3) the date on which the transaction will settle, called the delivery or final settlement date.

An important issue with futures is the ability to deliver or take delivery of the item contracted. Some financial responsibility is demanded. Here that means there is a 'margin' requirement – an amount of money that must be deposited and/or maintained in an account while the contract is in force. For example, if the margin requirement for corn is 10%, you could buy $100,000 worth of corn and deposit only $10,000. By delivery date you would have to sell the contract or come up with another $90,000 (and be ready to receive a whole bunch of corn).

Futures are used for a number of purposes. Farmers, miners, and others who extract or produce raw goods can lock in levels of income. Food manufacturers and industries of all kinds can lock in levels of costs. Futures can be a useful instrument for those who physically work with the items being traded. For people not involved with production or processing the underlying items, trading in futures is pure speculation with possibly disastrous consequences.

Why you should avoid futures

Massive loss potential

Given generous margin requirements that allow you to establish positions many times greater than your available capital, there is tremendous opportunity for massive loss. Taking the example above, if the price of corn falls 20% before the contract expires, this $100,000 future generates a loss of $20,000 to the buyer. Think of this: you deposit $10,000 for margin; you lose it all; and then you have to pay another $10,000 to cover the rest of the loss. After a 10% move in the underlying commodity, you lost 200% of the cash you invested.

Zero sum game

While all participants in the stock and bond markets can profit in the long run as economic growth leads to rising stock prices and payment of interest and dividends, futures contracts render no net profits. One party will make as much money as the other party loses. Futures are not investments; they are coin tosses.

Information disadvantage

Farmers and food processors, miners and manufacturers, investment bankers and financial engineers all study their markets intensely. Facing extreme potential for loss, futures buyers and sellers regularly employ expert meteorologists, geologists and math PhDs. A zero-sum game in which you are at a huge disadvantage with massive loss potential is not one you want to be playing.

Figure 14-1: Managed Futures vs Markets 2008-2017

——— Morningstar Managed Futures Fund Category Average

– – Vanguard 500 Index Fund

- - - Vanguard Total Bond Market Index Fund

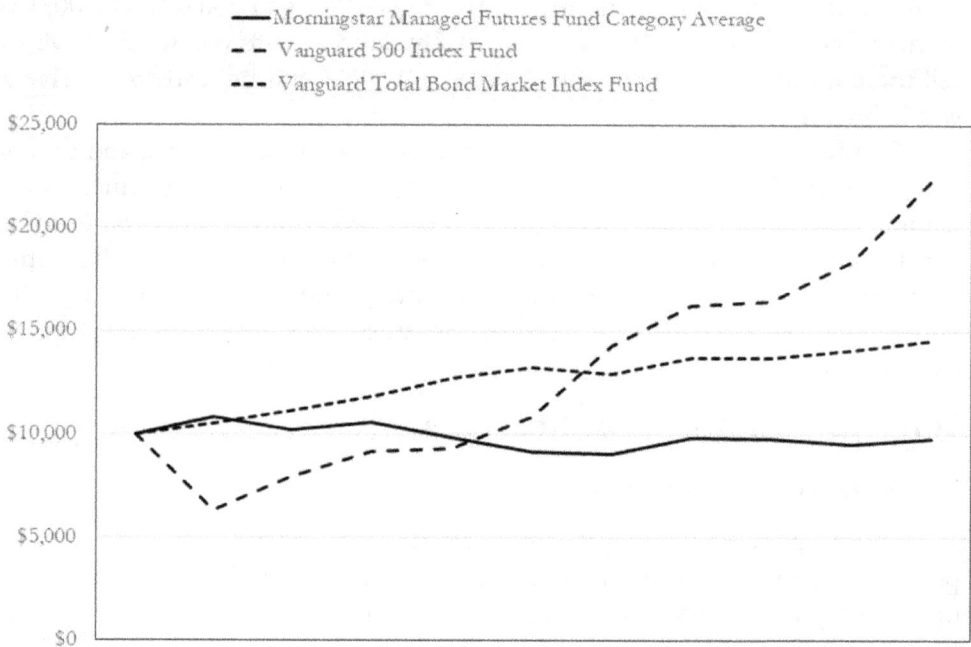

What you should do instead

If your interest in futures is high returns, this is not the right market. Huge risk would be added to your portfolio. In all likelihood returns would drop – perhaps to the point of financial ruin. Instead, reassess your risk tolerance. If you can handle a higher level of potential volatility, appropriately increase your exposure to stocks, reducing cash and bonds at the same time.

If your interest in futures stems from recent articles or research, know that experts who trade in the pertinent field read, perhaps even wrote, the same pieces. You are always at a disadvantage. Knowledgeable professionals already executed trades to move the markets before you finished reading. Facts and strong probabilities suggest you'll make more money in stocks and bonds than futures. Stick with the regular markets.

* Data sources:
The Vanguard Group, Inc., Morningstar, Inc.

15: Hedge Funds

What is a hedge fund?

A hedge fund is a legal entity which invests money gathered from its partners or shareholders – usually large chunks from wealthy individuals and/or institutions. Casual observers often confuse hedge funds with mutual funds, thinking the former a more advanced version of the latter. Such could not be farther from the truth.

Mutual funds are governed by the Investment Company Act of 1940. This act includes protections for investors, such as caps on expense rates, reporting requirements and third-party verification of assets.

Back in the 1940's some investors wanted to put their own money to work in a manner counter to the stock market. This new pool would thereby provide a 'hedge' to other assets, reducing overall volatility. To achieve this, behaviors not allowed by the Act of 1940 were needed. Set up outside the Act, the regulations protecting investors could also be ignored.

In the decades since, many more hedge funds have been created. Some attempt to hedge against certain markets; most were created to avoid regulations and extract exorbitant fee income through clever marketing.

Why you should avoid hedge funds

Ridiculously high fees

Free from the constraints of regulation, many hedge funds charge exorbitant fees. A typical fee structure might include a 2% fee on assets managed if returns are negative but a 20% to 35% cut of profits – even though it is your money that is completely at risk.

Bad upside / downside potential

Hedge fund fees are not just high; they are lopsided. When fund assets go down, investors get stuck with all the losses plus an additional 2% or so hit to assets for the fee. When fund assets go up, investors only receive 65% to 80% of the gain. By their very structure hedge funds render an unnaturally inferior risk-return tradeoff.

Figure 15-1 exhibits this tradeoff. The markets present a natural relationship between risk and return. Risk rises as higher returns are sought. It is a common analytical practice to plot portfolio returns against risk on a graph. Risk is usually an estimate of volatility such as standard deviation. Plotting all combinations of investments on the same chart generates a curve, often referred to as the efficient curve. Most combinations are below and to the right of the curve. The curve itself represents combinations in which returns are maximized at each level of risk.

Figure 15-1: Hedge Fund Fee Damage to Returns

- - Market/Index Fund Curve   ——Hedge Fund Curve Net of Fees

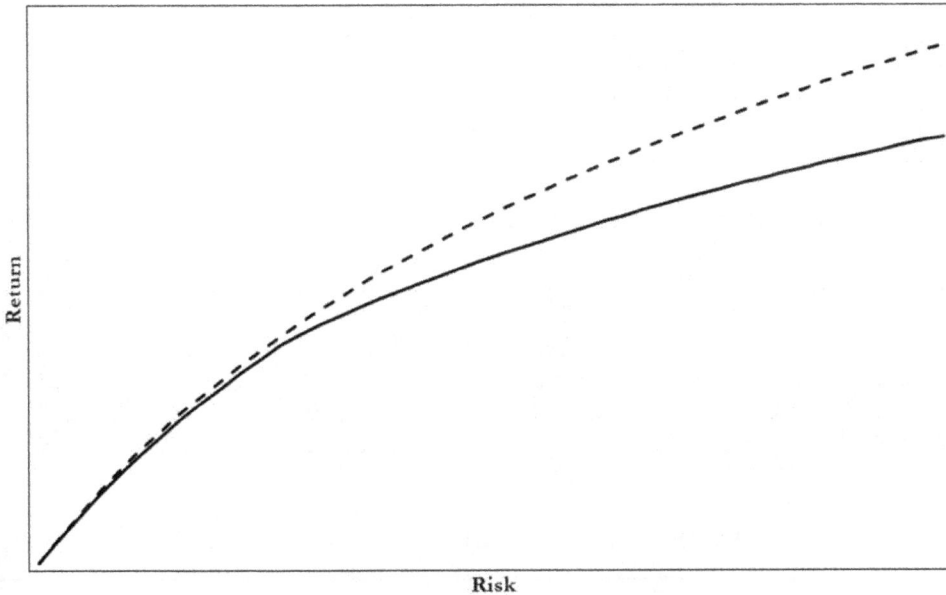

Granting hedge fund portfolios the benefit of returns that might be on the curve – which is a huge stretch since most hedge funds have not even come close to index returns – the design and excessive level of fees results in expected returns far below market levels for every level of risk accepted.

Imprudence

Hedge funds are not bound by regulation to maintain diversification or any other facet of rational investment behavior. Managers are free to do whatever they want with your money. Many attempt to achieve outsized returns through dangerously imprudent concentrations and derivatives. As headlines have shown, Bernie Madoff, Allen Stanford and others went further and took client money for themselves.

Lack of transparency

Though some hedge funds provide regular reports, they are not required to do so. With pricing and auditing often spotty, there is no assurance the assets purported to be held are in fact held. Mutual fund results are reported daily. Hedge fund results come out quarterly, often with huge surprises.

Figure 15-2: Hedge Fund Category Returns

Fund / Index Category	2017	5 Years 2013-17	10 Years 2008-17	15 Years 2003-17
Vanguard 500 Index Fund	21.67%	106.68%	123.44%	306.00%
Emerging Markets Hedge Fund Index	16.87%	34.55%	39.46%	243.32%
Long/Short Equity Hedge Fund Index	13.40%	40.91%	48.07%	176.27%
Long/Short Liquid Index	9.91%	37.56%	47.26%	176.36%
Equity Market Neutral Hedge Fund Index	8.45%	13.63%	-26.28%	8.35%
Event Driven Distressed Hedge Fund Index	7.30%	28.63%	46.06%	195.70%
Hedge Fund Index	7.13%	23.07%	37.53%	140.11%
Merger Arbitrage Liquid Index	6.83%	8.60%	17.17%	83.09%
Multi-Strategy Hedge Fund Index	6.83%	36.65%	60.90%	169.87%
Fixed Income Arbitrage Hedge Fund Index	6.52%	21.07%	43.53%	87.94%
Event Driven Hedge Fund Index	6.29%	19.99%	34.60%	163.96%
Event Driven Liquid Index	6.12%	18.68%	48.58%	171.22%
Event Driven Multi-Strategy Hedge Fund Index	5.87%	16.67%	29.97%	153.25%
Event Driven Risk Arbitrage Hedge Fund Index	5.79%	16.44%	34.86%	87.96%
Convertible Arbitrage Hedge Fund Index	5.00%	17.65%	43.51%	93.53%
Liquid Alternative Beta Index	4.64%	21.23%	34.75%	134.95%
Managed Futures Hedge Fund Index	3.29%	9.95%	26.84%	75.54%
Global Strategies Liquid Index	2.62%	18.74%	25.85%	102.92%
Global Macro Hedge Fund Index	2.14%	13.97%	53.09%	185.29%
Managed Futures Liquid Index	-2.26%	31.25%	49.83%	161.65%
Dedicated Short Bias Hedge Fund Index	-2.99%	-41.51%	-67.70%	-76.73%

Poor Performance

In the book "The Hedge Fund Mirage" (John Wiley & Sons, Hoboken, NJ, 2012), author Simon Lack reports 84% of all the gains earned by all hedge funds between 1998 and 2010 went to the managers of those funds; investors in hedge funds during those same years kept 16% of the gains. Basically, investors paid through their nose to entrust money with famous managers only to earn a fraction of what they would have garnered with index mutual funds.

Figure 15-2 reveals a stunning perspective. Average hedge fund returns in every category monitored by Credit Suisse underperformed index funds tracking the Standard & Poor's 500 in 2017 as well as the past five years, ten years, and fifteen years. They may be rich, famous and connected; but as a whole modern hedge fund managers are demonstrably among the worst investors ever entrusted with other people's money. Stay clear.

What you should do instead

If you already hold a stake in a hedge fund, you may want to act now to withdraw your money. If you are considering a new purchase, lose the thought.

If you seek a specific investment exposure of a particular hedge fund but through a superior vehicle in terms of cost, risk-reward, safety and liquidity, choose a regulated ETF or mutual fund with similar goals. If hedge funds are the centerpiece of your investment regimen, consider a new one. Read Section IV.

* Data sources:
The Vanguard Group, Inc., Credit Suisse Hedge Index LLC.
Hedge fund fees modeled assume 25% of returns in excess of 6%, with a 2% minimum.

16: IPOs of Stocks

What is an initial public offering (IPO)?

An initial public offering (IPO) is the first public sale of a security.

IPOs occur all the time in the debt markets as governments and large corporations who borrow money usually do so by issuing new bonds. If you are already comfortable with the borrowing entity, a new issue bond can be an effective way to earn a better than average yield. You should only consider participating in a bond IPO if you would otherwise have bought the same bond had it already been in existence at the offered yield. If you have access to a decent bond platform you can readily navigate to listings of new bonds for sale. Chapter 49 contains pointers on selecting bonds, new or outstanding.

Stock IPOs are the ones that make the news. In fact, when the press and public speak of IPOs, they are usually referring to stocks. Even casual news readers probably know those who bought Apple or Google stock during their IPOs made a fortune while those who bought Vonage lost most of their money and those with Pets.com lost their entire investment.

Why you should avoid stock IPOs

Naturally bad timing

Company officials know better than investors when they can get a good price for their stock. They know when sales have been better than usual; when the company's gone a long time without any negative events; when favorable publicity might augment perception of worth. Current shareholders of private companies are not forced to sell anything, and yet at the time of an IPO they have decided to sell shares in something of which they have total knowledge. If you have something to sell, would you sell it at a time when its price is high or when you are pretty sure you're not going to get a fair deal? Of course you'd choose an opportune time. Companies are no different.

Consider the data graphed in Figure 16-1. In a comprehensive survey of IPOs executed over more than four decades, Professor Jay R. Ritter at the University of Florida found that IPOs underperformed already outstanding stocks of equivalently capitalized firms by 3.4% annually over the following five years. When equivalent book value was added as a requirement for comparison, IPOs underperformed by 2.1% annually.

Fees that reduce value

When stock is issued via an IPO, net of fees to the investment banker, the money spent buying new shares goes into the corporate balance sheet.

Money spent to buy outstanding shares goes to former holders of those shares.

Despite reduced costs of office work and communications, high investment banking fees have stuck. For every dollar you spend for new stock, the firm issuing the stock gets perhaps 93 to 97 cents. Of course, shares sold by current holders in an IPO generate no new funds for the company. You are rewarding investment bankers and insiders at a price they set. You are not effectively funding operations of some new discovery.

Figure 16-1: 5-Year Returns - IPOs vs Non-IPOs

▣ Initial Public Offerings
▨ Firms Already Public with the Same Market Cap
▦ Initial Public Offerings with Book Value and Market Cap Matches
▥ Firms Already Public with the Same Market Cap and Book Value

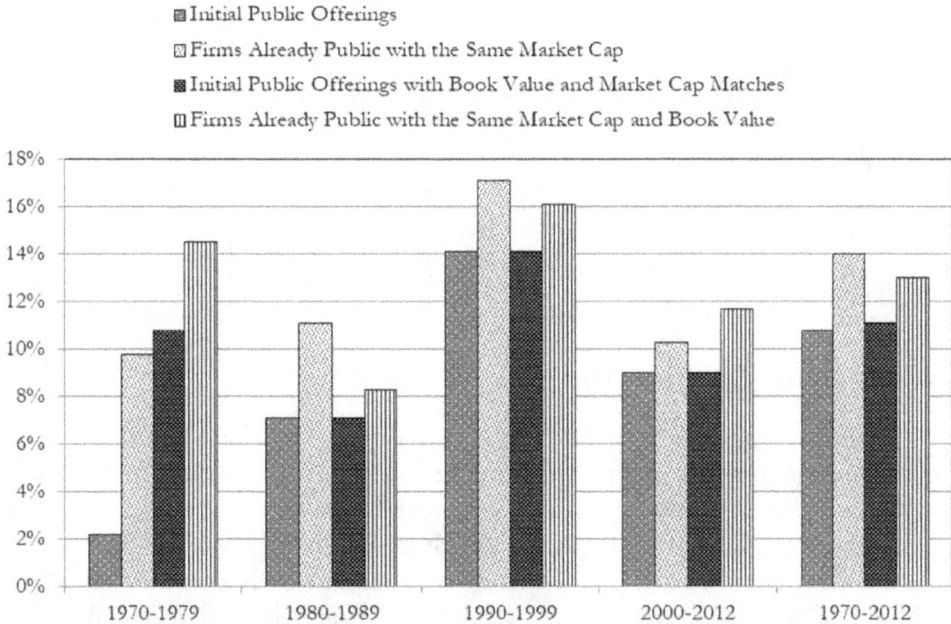

Fees that provide evil intentions

IPO fees are so lucrative they provide incentive for deals not warranted by the issuing company's goals and interests. Many IPOs are simply the result of fee-greedy investment bankers bribing company officials with huge stakes and payouts, all funded by new investors. Further, IPO fees are vastly greater than brokerage commissions. During the period that IPO shares are being marketed, brokers earn far more serving the interests of their investment banking clients than they do serving your interest.

Unfavorably lopsided share allotments

During their respective IPOs, most orders for Google were allotted fewer shares than requested while almost everyone who ordered Facebook got every share asked for. Of course, Google skyrocketed and Facebook plummeted over the next few months. The allocation was not a coincidence or a mistake. If a deal is "hot", as in the case of Google, favored clients and insiders will get preferential treatment and receive the lion's share of allotments. Regular folk like you will be left out in the cold, perhaps getting a fraction of what you ask for, if any. If a deal is not well received, perhaps doomed for quick decline, the general public will be unaware while insiders and institutions will be warned. In these situations regular investors like you will get every share requested.

Figure 16-2: IPO Comparable Returns Following Day of Issuance

	1970-1979	1980-1989	1990-1999	2000-2012	1970-2012
Initial Public Offerings	2.20%	7.10%	14.10%	9.00%	10.80%
Firms Already Public with the Same Market Cap	9.80%	11.10%	17.10%	10.30%	14.00%
Initial Public Offerings with Book Value and Market Cap Matches	10.80%	7.10%	14.10%	9.00%	11.10%
Firms Already Public with the Same Market Cap and Book Value	14.50%	8.30%	16.10%	11.70%	13.00%

What you should do instead

Unless you are an insider who can legally discern tangibly positive relative value in a new issue, you should avoid the IPO market. If you like the nature of the IPO issuing firm's business, consider a low expense index exchange traded fund that focuses on that industry. If you are intrigued by the specific details of that company, continue to follow it after the initial shares are placed. Investors who bought Google (or IBM, or Apple, or Facebook) weeks, months and even years after the IPO did very well.

* Data source:
Professor Jay R. Ritter, University of Florida, "Returns on IPOs during the five years after issuing, for IPOs from 1970-2013", 2014.

17: Master Limited Partnerships

What is a master limited partnership?

A master limited partnership (MLP) is a company whose partnership units (of ownership) trade like common stock shares of public corporations. General partners operate the enterprise and limited partners provide the money for the general partners to use.

The goal, like most corporations, is to generate profits. Unlike most corporations, master limited partnerships do not pay taxes at the corporate level. Profits and losses are reported to partners who add their pro-rata portion of the income (or subtract the losses) in the course of handling personal income taxes. MLPs must generate at least 90% of their revenues from real estate or extraction related industries such as oil and commodities.

MLP dividend yields are usually higher than the average of common stocks. Meanwhile the favorable corporate tax treatment is of great benefit to those who operate in the allowable industries. For several years, MLPs profited from a long-term decline in interest rates and a rise in energy prices. They also benefited from increased demand as some Wall Street firms created MLP-focused funds to capitalize on recent, if moot, past performance.

Why you should avoid master limited partnerships

Tax complications

Tax related data for most investments is usually gathered and conveniently reported by the institutions where securities are held. MLP tax related data is accessed through the MLP. If you own units of five MLPs, you must go to five websites and submit your Social Security number to obtain the required tax related documents.

Further, while income and capital gains info for stocks, bonds and funds are available just after the end of the year, MLPs cannot report results until they are fully audited. This process can go well into the following year. Owners of MLPs often have to file tax extensions and/or amended returns.

Moreover, MLPs require additional IRS paperwork. If you do your own taxes, you will likely add several hours to your preparation time. If you have someone else do your taxes, you will probably be charged substantially more just for the MLP related work.

Disappointing Net Returns

Accounting costs and difficulties aside, the level of MLP taxation can bring unwelcome surprises. Because MLPs are not taxed at the corporate level, owners of MLP shares have the burden of reporting and paying taxes on operational income. This is in addition to whatever investment income and realized appreciation are earned and reported.

This tax reduces returns. Most sales presentations pushing MLPs and funds consisting of MLPs emphasize dividend yields that are higher than other income-oriented vehicles. But after accounting for taxes, the net returns are nothing to brag about.

Compounding matters further, at a relatively low threshold, operational income from MLPs can become reportable and taxable in otherwise tax-exempt accounts like IRAs.

Industry concentration

MLPs must be predominantly real estate or natural resource operations. A substantial commitment to these securities could bring about unwanted industry concentration.

What you should do instead

If your interest in MLPs stems from a desire for yield, you can increase income in more efficacious ways. Among equities, you can shift assets toward stocks and index funds that pay higher than average dividends. Utilities, telecommunications and older firms with solid product lines often have excellent payouts, as do funds with the moniker "value". Within the bond arena, there are ways to augment yield, such as extending maturity or loosening credit standards.

If you sought MLPs to invest in real estate, oil or other commodities, index funds focused in these industries will provide you with the desired, diversified exposure without the negatives of MLPs.

Lastly, since worth rises with growth as well as income, you may want to temper your quest for yield and think longer term. Put another way, implementing a healthy overall regimen will save you time and energy while serving your long-term wealth. This route is easier and more fruitful than involvement with complicated corporate structures such as MLPs. Read Section IV for more guidance.

18: Mutual Funds You Should Avoid

What is a mutual fund?

A mutual fund is an investment company, a firm whose primary operation is managing a portfolio of securities. Shareholders own, pro-rata, a portion of the entire portfolio. The portfolio must conform to restrictions set forth in the fund's prospectus. A fund required to hold stocks in the Standard & Poor's 500 Index will hold such; a shareholder of the fund will thereby own tiny amounts of these S&P 500 stocks.

Mutual funds are priced at the end of each trading day. The market values of all securities held are tabulated using their closing prices. Other assets such as cash and accrued interest are added while liabilities such as fees payable are subtracted. The result is called the net asset value (NAV). This amount is divided by the number of shares outstanding to produce the NAV per share. For no-load mutual funds – the only type you should ever consider – this NAV is also the share price. All new purchases and sales of fund shares placed since the last business day will transact using this newly calculated price.

Mutual funds present an excellent means to obtain instant diversification. You can build a portfolio with one broadly invested fund or use multiple funds with exposure in specific sectors and security types. Helpful pointers to select optimally effective mutual funds are outlined in Section IV.

Funds You Should Avoid

Despite instant diversification and noble stated goals, a host of ignoble features have proliferated throughout the mutual fund arena. High fees, imprudent positions, limited visibility and unacceptable risk can crush investor returns. Wall Street perpetually creates products to nominally address particular needs and take advantage of fads. Common sales pitches, like good recent performance or focus on a hot sector, are boldly printed and colorfully displayed on the web. Grimy details, such as sales charges and periods of poor performance, are hidden deep in prospectuses and disclosure statements.

Though any generic fund can exhibit lackluster behavior, there are whole categories of funds whose very designs are red flags. The following 12 chapters provide details on major fund categories you should avoid. They are summarized in Figure 18-1.

Figure 18-1: Mutual Funds You Should Avoid

Chapter	Fund Type	Sales Fees	No Expected Growth	Structural Problems	High Fees or Risk for Returns Sought
19	Asset allocation			Y	Y
20	Bear Market		Y	Y	
21	Bond			Y	Y
22	Currency		Y	Y	
23	Funds of funds			Y	Y
24	Loaded Mutual	Y			Y
25	Loaded A-Share	Y			Y
26	Loaded B-Share	Y			Y
27	Loaded C-Share	Y			Y
28	Long/Short			Y	Y
29	Managed			Y	Y
30	Target Date			Y	Y

19: Mutual Funds: Asset Allocation Funds

What is an asset allocation fund?

An asset allocation fund is a mutual fund with both stocks and bonds presented as a one-stop shopping solution to your portfolio management needs. While some such funds use the words "balanced" or "equity income" in their names, many get right to the point and use terms like "conservative", "moderate" or "aggressive". The selling point of such funds is the ease with which you can find a fund whose name suggests suitability to your risk profile.

Some asset allocation funds have teams of portfolio managers who analyze and select individual stocks and bonds. Many invest in other mutual funds; usually one or more stock funds and one or more bond funds. In general, conservative allocation funds will have a higher percentage of assets invested in bonds than stocks. Aggressive allocation funds will emphasize stocks. Moderate funds sit between the other two in terms of allocation.

Why you should avoid asset allocation funds

Lack of flexibility

If you devote all assets to an asset allocation fund, regardless of what you might feel about the markets or world, the allocation of your assets is set by formula. You have no control. In fact, even if you decide to pay higher fees to own allocation fund shares guided by a professional money manager, that manager also has scant control over the asset allocation.

High fees for service provided

Asset allocation funds consist of both stocks and bonds. Although bonds involve less active management and usually incur lower fees, most asset allocation funds charge high equity-level expense rates for the entire balance. Further, many asset allocation products are "funds of funds" (Chapter 23). They achieve their target allocations by shifting money between stock and bond funds, engendering multiple layers of fees and lack of transparency.

What you should do instead

If you know enough to pick an allocation fund, you know enough to allocate your assets. If you lean toward a conservative allocation fund, consider putting between 70% and 80% of your assets in bonds or bond funds and the rest (20%-30%) in stocks or stock funds. If you're on the aggressive side, reverse that mix. If you are moderate, keep both stocks and bonds in the 40% to 60% range. As time passes, your results and reactions to them may help you refine your percentages toward the upper or lower end of those ranges.

Since asset allocation funds are presented as holistic one stop solutions, the superior replacement strategy is a rational investment program. Read Section IV.

20: Mutual Funds: Bear Market Funds

What is a bear market fund?

A bear market fund is a mutual fund whose goal is to go up when the market goes down. At worst, these funds aim to outperform the market during declines, perhaps falling as well but by a lower percentage.

Why you should avoid bear market funds

Markets generally rise

In their pure form, bear market funds seek results that are opposite the market. Of course, when you invest, you seek growth. Despite crashes and panics, the market rises over time. Putting your money in a bear market fund is a bet against history, one that has failed every investment cycle. Figure 20-1 compares the change in value of stock and bond index funds and the average of all bear market funds tracked by Morningstar. During a decade that included one of the worst bear markets ever, bear market funds lost over 85% of their value.

You would pay two fees for nothing

Assuming you would not put all of your money in a bear market fund, what about 'hedging' a little, holding a bear market fund while you also hold stocks or regular stock funds? Don't. Each fund will charge fees. For every dollar invested in both, the net expected return is about zero, minus those fees. It is a ridiculous combination. It would be more effective to hold cash.

Market timing is a bad tactic

Since bear market funds are doomed to fail in the long run, what about short horizons when markets go down? If you know when the market will rise and fall, by all means take advantage. Unfortunately, no one knows. Market timing sounds like a great tactic, but even professionals cannot do it profitably (Chapter 42). What are your chances?

Derivatives are bad instruments

To move opposite the market, bear market funds must hold short positions (Chapter 40) and/or derivatives (Chapter 12). Aside from the benefits of diversification, a fund is no better than the sum of its parts. If the parts are faulty, the fund is faulty. Volatility, withering value and participation in negative sum games are the building blocks of bear funds. You would not buy these instruments directly. You should not buy them through a fund.

Figure 20-1: Bear Funds vs Markets 2008-2017

—— Morningstar Bear Fund Category Average

– – Vanguard 500 Index Fund

- - - Vanguard Total Bond Market Index Fund

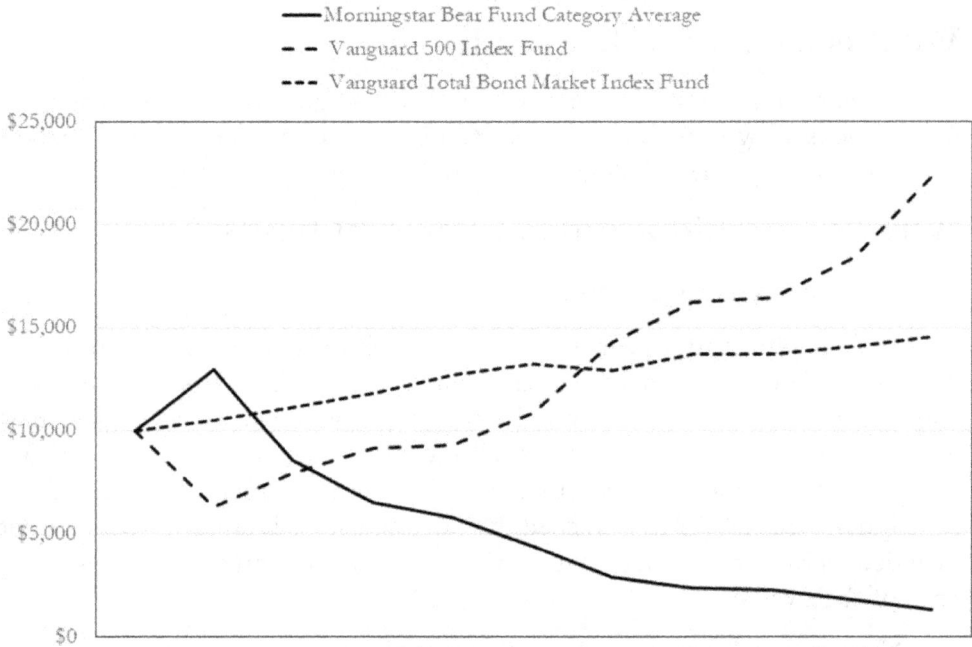

What you should do instead

First, do not try to time the market. If you are considering a bear market fund, you are probably worried about a major market decline. If your fear is at all fleeting or based on scant evidence, resist the temptation and move on.

If instead your concern is palpable and deep, it is possible your risk profile has shifted. You may want to reassess your tolerance. Moving toward a more conservative posture may make sense. If so, reduce your stock holdings and either put more to work in bonds or let the proceeds from stock sales sit in cash until your tolerance shifts back in the other direction. Read Chapter 45 for help assessing your current risk profile.

* Data sources:
The Vanguard Group, Inc., Morningstar, Inc.

21: Mutual Funds: Bond Funds

What is a bond mutual fund?

Bond mutual funds are mutual funds invested in fixed income instruments. Usually bond funds will focus on a particular segment of the market, such as short-term government bonds, high yield corporate bonds, municipal bonds, and so forth.

Low cost no-load bond mutual funds might make sense for many small investors. As with all mutual funds, you gain immediate diversification. This is especially important with corporate bonds, since there is some risk of default (missed payments). If a bond default occurs in a mutual fund, shareholders barely notice. If a default occurs among the few bonds that would be held in a small personal portfolio, the loss could be devastating.

Further, funds have the convenience of practically unlimited unit size. Bonds are usually bought in round amounts. Most have a face value of $1,000. To defray costs and obtain maximal yields, moreover, bonds are often bought in blocks of $5,000 or more. Meanwhile, most bond mutual funds allow incremental additions and withdrawals of practically any dollar amount.

However, once you have more than a critical minimum, perhaps $10,000 to $20,000, you may be better served owning CDs and bonds directly instead of bond funds.

Why you should avoid bond funds (once you can buy bonds)

Expenses

Bonds are purchased primarily for income. Fund expenses detract from that income. Many managed bond funds charge around 1% for management. These fees represent a substantial portion of the income earned on most fixed income instruments. Using low cost no-load bond funds can keep expenses low. Buying bonds directly can wipe them out.

Lack of maturity

When you buy a bond, assuming the issuer is financially sound, you will receive the face value (usually $1,000) of that bond at maturity. Your rate of return will be exactly equal to the yield-to-maturity you secured when you bought the bond. Whether interest rates go up or down, and regardless of other factors that affect market prices during the period of ownership, at maturity you will get the face amount.

When you buy bond mutual fund shares, the value of those shares will rise and fall in the opposite direction of interest rate moves. Share prices will also change due to events affecting issuers of bonds held in the fund. Any good news and marginally bad news can change prices a little; devastating news like bankruptcy can cause great damage. The bottom line: unlike bonds, bond funds present an unknown rate of return.

Figure 21-1 models the growth of $10,000 over a 20-year period with changing interest rates. Assume the rate on a 5-year bond starts at 4%, rises by 0.25% annually for five years, drops 0.25% annually for the following ten years, then rises again, returning to 4% in year 20. The individual bond line reflects the purchase of a 5-year bond at 4% with reinvestment of all proceeds – interest payments and maturing principal – into new 5-year bonds at the new "current" interest rate. The bond fund line reflects the purchase of shares of a mutual fund whose only assets are 5-year bonds bought under the same circumstances as the individual bond line. A fund expense ratio of 0.5% is assumed.

As seen in the graph, the drain of fees and price volatility cause the fund to generate about $2,300 less return – a sacrifice of 23% of the initial investment though invested in identical market circumstances.

Figure 21-1: Bonds vs Bond Funds - 20 Year Model

- - Individual Bonds ——Bond Fund

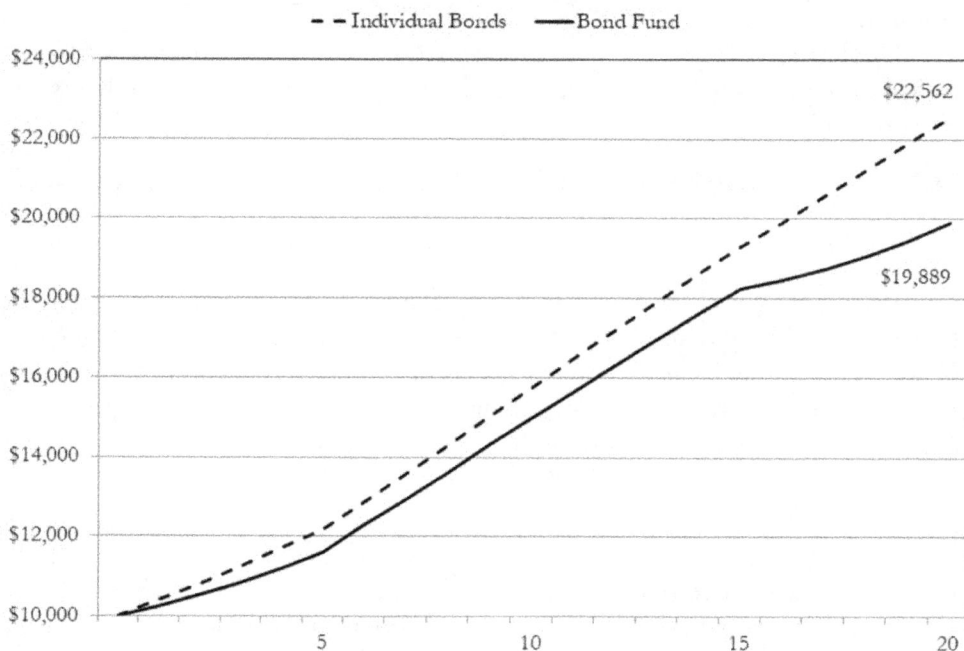

Adverse behavior

Most investors follow the herd when there is widely broadcast news. Bad reports often lead to panic; popular trends often lead to hype. Mutual fund investors have been notoriously guilty of acting with the herd mentality.

After price declines show up on statements investors often express their disappointment by liquidating their mutual fund shares. Conversely, when news arises about huge returns in a particular fund or market segment, many investors jump on board.

Mutual fund portfolio managers have to invest when deposits are received, and they must sell holdings when liquidations occur. Combining this fact with the herd mentality of shareholders, bond funds tend to add positions in times of lower yields and higher prices; they commonly have to sell after prices fall, when yields are higher. Buying high and selling low does not work well for anybody.

Unknown tax consequences

If you buy a bond, the tax consequences are known. Interest is taxed while the difference between the price paid and the amount received at maturity will either add to or be deducted from income.

When you buy mutual fund shares, your ultimate tax liability is uncertain. Future liquidations of fund shares will be executed at prices not yet know. You may have losses, reducing the benefit of interest earned; you may have gains which will be taxed. Meanwhile, during the period you hold fund shares, if the portfolio manager sells bonds at a gain or loss, those gains and losses will be passed on to you with tax consequences.

What you should do instead

Because of the negative attributes highlighted above, you should only invest in bond funds when forced by circumstance. For instance, many retirement plan platforms are comprised solely of mutual funds. Maybe a specific account does not have enough money to buy a decent yielding CD or bond. Whatever the limitation, minimize your expenses and select a fund comprised of bonds you would buy individually.

For the rest of your fixed income investing, buy bonds and CDs. Chapter 49 provides gainful suggestions for building a solid portfolio. Assuming you stick with securities from creditworthy issuers you will know the forthcoming rate of return of each position; a return unhindered by expense, undamaged by herd mentality, and uncomplicated by unforeseen tax consequences.

22: Mutual Funds: Currency Funds

What is a currency fund?

A currency fund is a mutual fund consisting of foreign currencies and securities denominated in foreign currencies. The fund can hold actual money but more likely will invest in money market instruments and futures contracts (Chapter 14).

Why you should avoid currency funds

They are not an investment

Currency is not an investment. Like the dollar, the money of foreign countries is a medium of exchange to facilitate transactions, a unit of measure through which we ascribe value, and a store of wealth which can be accumulated. There is no reason to expect any growth or earnings. Since cash equivalent securities are often held, a small return akin to money market rates may be achieved. But after expenses are accounted for, currency funds are quite likely to provide negative returns.

Figure 22-1: Currency Funds vs Markets 2008-2017

——— Morningstar Currency Fund Category Average

– – Vanguard 500 Index Fund

--- Vanguard Total Bond Market Index Fund

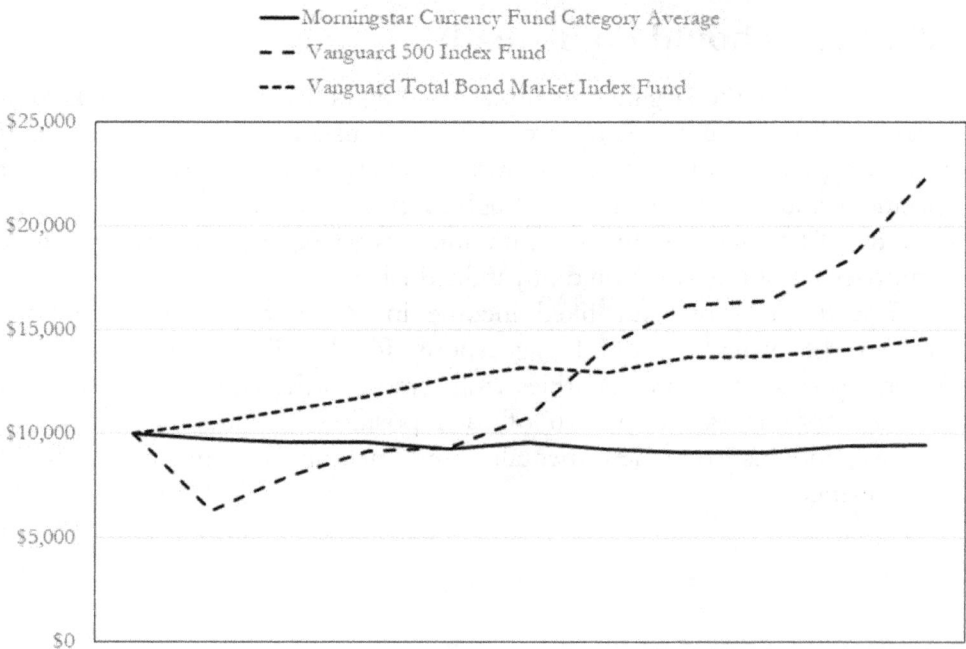

They are a gamble

Exchange rates vary over time for a variety of economic and political reasons. There are many thousands of currency traders, some who do it for speculation, others as a course of business related to international trade and finance. The massive buying and selling of these participants results in the exchange rates we see posted online and in the papers. All the information known at any given time is reflected in these rates. If you think you know more than these participants, think again. At best you are looking at a coin toss. You bet heads. Expect tails. As you can see in Figure 22-1, during the decade ending 2017 the average return of all professionally managed currency funds was negative.

What you should do instead

If your interest in currency funds is based purely on the notion of appreciation, devote those dollars to the equity markets. Even if the dollar declines in value relative to other currencies, as long as you spend the bulk of your money in the U.S. you are no worse off. Moreover, a declining dollar makes American goods seem cheaper abroad. Expanding sales of U.S. made merchandise is good for U.S. stock prices.

If your interest in currency funds is based on a favorable impression of certain foreign economies, invest in the stocks of foreign companies instead. Profit seeking enterprises operating abroad should serve your needs better than a pile of stagnant cash. Seek no-load index mutual funds and low-cost exchange traded funds focused in the desired country or region.

* Data sources:
The Vanguard Group, Inc., Morningstar, Inc.

23: Mutual Funds: Funds of Funds

What is a fund of funds?

Most mutual funds build diversified portfolios of individual stocks, bonds, and other securities. A mutual fund of funds instead invests in other funds.

Usually, a fund of funds is created to implement a particular asset allocation strategy. For instance, target date funds shift assets from stocks toward bonds over time, getting more conservative as shareholders get closer to retirement. These funds can periodically sell many individual stocks and buy many bonds; instead they could just sell shares of one stock fund and buy shares of one bond fund.

Why you should avoid funds of funds

Uncontrolled asset allocation

When you invest in a fund of funds you surrender control of your own asset allocation to another party. Your tolerance for risk should determine the percentages of your portfolio devoted to stocks and bonds. Funds of funds may indicate targets, but in practice they can deviate out of line with your own preference or risk tolerance.

After you put the effort into determining an appropriate asset allocation, you should not introduce doubt during its execution.

Figure 23-1: Effect on Returns of a Fund of Funds

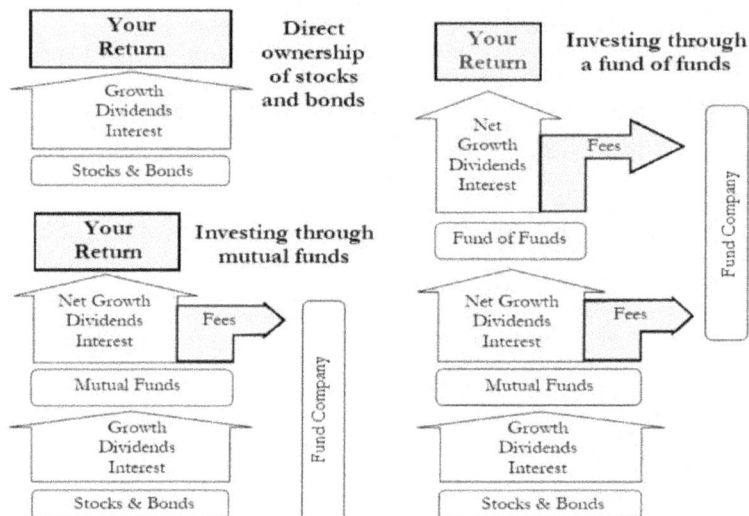

Layers of fees

All mutual funds charge fees. Some funds of funds offset fees of the mutual funds they purchase to prevent double billing. Many do not.

Piling on fees impedes performance. Figure 23-1 demonstrates the process. Basically, stocks and bonds generate income and growth. Each level of product that comes between you and those stocks and bonds will detract from your portfolio's performance.

Fund family bias

Some funds of funds research targeted market segments seeking 'best in breed' selections. Many funds of funds utilize products in the same fund family. Instead of finding the best stock and bond funds, these in-house funds of funds are forced to invest in the stock and bond funds managed by related parties regardless of fees or merit.

Reduced transparency

Mutual funds regularly provide portfolio details that include lists of securities. For funds of funds, these lists will include the names of funds, not the stocks and bonds ultimately held. While it is not impossible to get those details, it takes extra work.

What you should do instead

Is your fund of funds a target date fund? See Chapter 30 for more context and corrective action.

Is your fund of funds risk related, with an emphasis on aggressiveness, conservatism or moderation? Read Chapter 19 for perspective and actionable ideas.

If you own or are considering a fund of funds as a one-stop solution to your investing needs, execute a proper investment regimen instead. Section IV lays out an easy path to such a regimen.

24: Mutual Funds: Loaded Mutual Funds

What is a loaded mutual fund?

A loaded mutual fund is a mutual fund whose shares can only be acquired by paying sales charges. These charges might be collected up front at the time of purchase, later on upon sale, or daily during ownership. Loads have nothing to do with fund management, fund administration or service. Plain and simple, these fees are commissions paid to salespeople who make no contribution to your financial improvement.

Years ago, loaded mutual funds were the predominant way individuals acquired diversified portfolios. With neither computers nor access to the exchanges, investors had to deal with local representatives. Sales fees charged for loaded funds were an accepted cost of distribution.

With easy access to the internet, fund companies and discount brokers, you can buy shares of no-load mutual funds and other cost-efficient vehicles as easily as books and shoes. There is no reason to waste away your assets shelling out commissions. When you have a major problem with a sink you call a plumber. You don't pay a salesperson to send the plumber.

Over the years, Wall Street has become ever more creative in finding new ways to charge and hide fees. The next three chapters address the most common forms of loaded funds: A-, B-, and C-shares.

25: Mutual Funds: Loaded A-Share Funds

What is an A-share mutual fund?

An A-share mutual fund, also known as a front-end loaded mutual fund, incurs a sales charge at purchase. If the load is 6%, your investment of $10,000 will leave you $9,400 worth of shares at the end of the first day. Some misleading firms use the phrases "bid" and "ask" as if mutual funds trade like stock. They do not. In those quotes, the lower "bid" price is equal to the net asset value of the portfolio, just like the price of a no-load fund. The higher "ask" price adds the sales charge. When you buy shares, you must pay this higher price.

Why you should avoid loaded A-share mutual funds

Immediate loss of value

Paying a front-end load immediately reduces your wealth. For example, spending $50,000 on a fund with a 6% load leaves you with $47,000 as of the first day. Your investment must grow by about 6.4% just to get back to $50,000 – where you'd have been had you simply stuffed your money in a pillow case instead.

Figure 25-1: A-Share vs No-Load Stock Funds 1998-2017

——Loaded A-Share　　－ －No Load

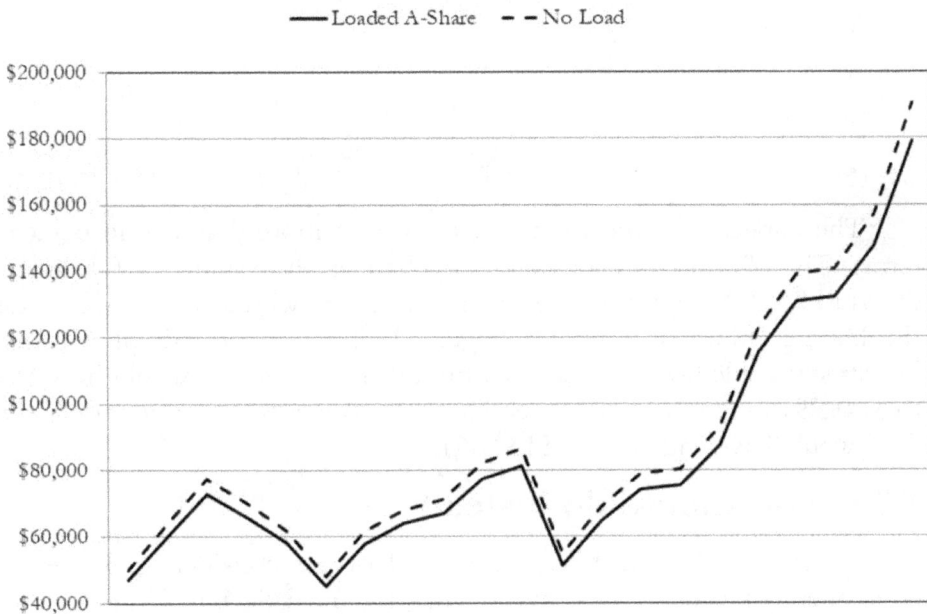

Permanent and increasing harm

As investments grow over time the magnitude of forfeited money grows as well. A $50,000 investment in a no-load index fund tracking the S&P 500 with a 0.2% expense ratio at the start of 1998 would have grown to $190,613 by the end of 2017. If a 6% loaded fund was purchased instead, the $47,000 of identically invested assets would have grown to $179,176. Invested in the same stocks, the $3,000 loss from sales fees grew to over $10,000.

Figure 25-2: A-Share vs No-Load Bond Funds 1998-2017

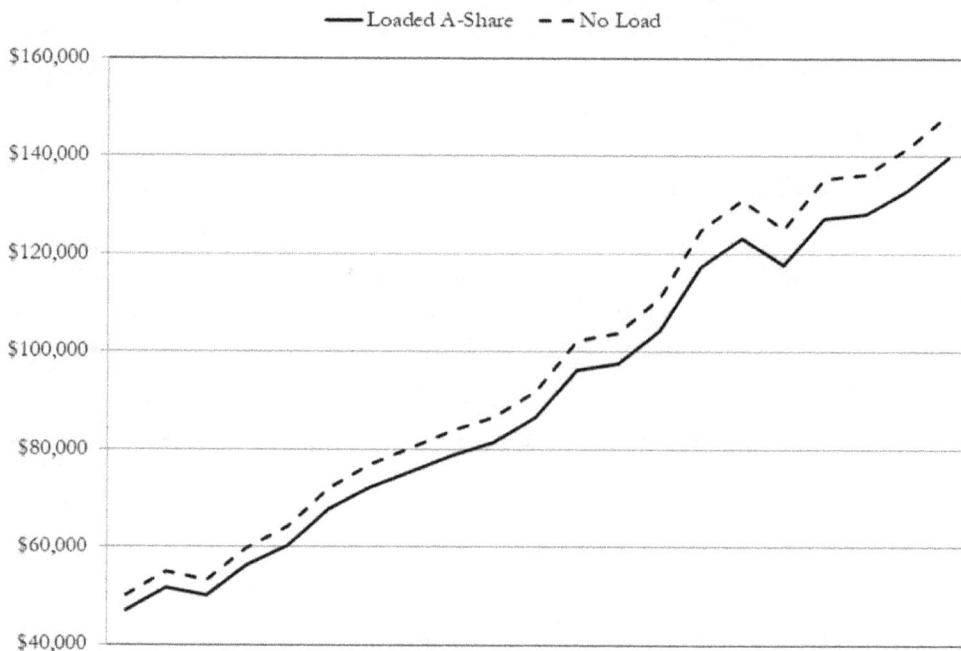

The impact on bond fund returns is even more dramatic in percentage terms. The 6% hit to your initial purchase is the same; $50,000 instantly drops to $47,000. But when stripped from assets with lower average returns, the harm is more pronounced. Figure 25-2 shows growth of a blend of investment grade bonds. A no-load fund with these assets would have grown to $148,791 in the two decades ending 2017. A loaded but otherwise identical fund would have ended up at $139,864.

What you should do instead

If the loaded mutual fund you hold or are considering is the major component of your overall investment plan, read Section IV for a proper investment regimen.

If instead you hold or are considering a loaded mutual fund as a specific 'solution', such as handling your mid-cap exposure, find a low-cost no-load fund in the same category. Morningstar and good institutional platforms have handy mutual fund screening tools. Sort by expense ratio; index funds within the category will likely be at the top of the list. If there are no low-cost index funds at your institution, you should switch institutions (Chapter 47).

* Data sources:
Stock returns: S&P Dow Jones Indices LLC; Standard & Poor's 500 Index.
Bond returns: Federal Reserve Release H-15; An index of equal parts (25% each) Moody's Aaa corporate bonds, Moody's Baa corporate bonds, 5-year Treasury bonds, and 10-year Treasury bonds, rebalanced annually.
Fund expense rate: 0.2%
Loaded A-share sales charge: 6% upon purchase.

26: Mutual Funds: Loaded B-Share Funds

What is a B-share mutual fund?

B-share mutual funds have sales charges as high as A-shares, but they hit in a less obvious fashion. For years, reps faced resistance from prospective clients who objected to the immediate loss of money after purchasing front-loaded A-shares. Promoting investments guaranteeing a substantial loss on day one is a hard sale. B-shares were designed to overcome the visibility of this defect, though not the defect itself.

To pay the sales folks, B-shares add a charge to the fund's other expenses, taking a little bit every day for commissions. A 6% load might be collected at the rate of 1% per year for six years, or 0.75% for eight years, or some other pace and length that strips at least 6%. To ensure the whole commission gets collected, B-shares add a back-end penalty. If a B-share owner sells shares before the entire sales fee has been paid, the proceeds from the share liquidation are reduced by an amount roughly equal to the uncollected commissions. A typical back-end penalty structure might stipulate a 6% charge the first year of ownership, a 5% charge the second year, a 4% hit the third year and so on until the penalty disappears in year seven.

Figure 26-1: B-Share vs No-Load Stock Funds 1998-2017

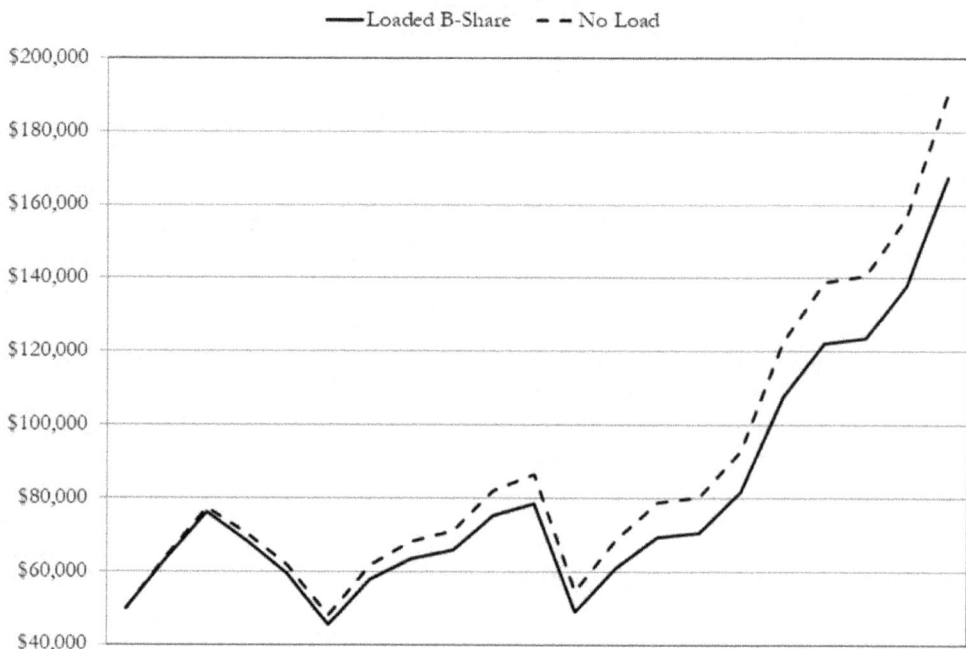

——Loaded B-Share − − No Load

Why you should avoid B-share mutual funds

High annual charges

Just like other mutual funds, B-share funds incur management and administrative expenses. B-share commissions known as 12b-1 fees are added to this, creating a huge total expense ratio. It is not uncommon for annual B-share fees to amount to 2% or more. This can completely wipe out the returns of many bond funds and it's a major hit to stock returns as well. The commission drainage eventually ends, often after six or seven years. But it starts again on newly deposited money and re-invested dividends.

Figure 26-2: B-Share vs No-Load Bond Funds 1998-2017

——Loaded B-Share   – – No Load

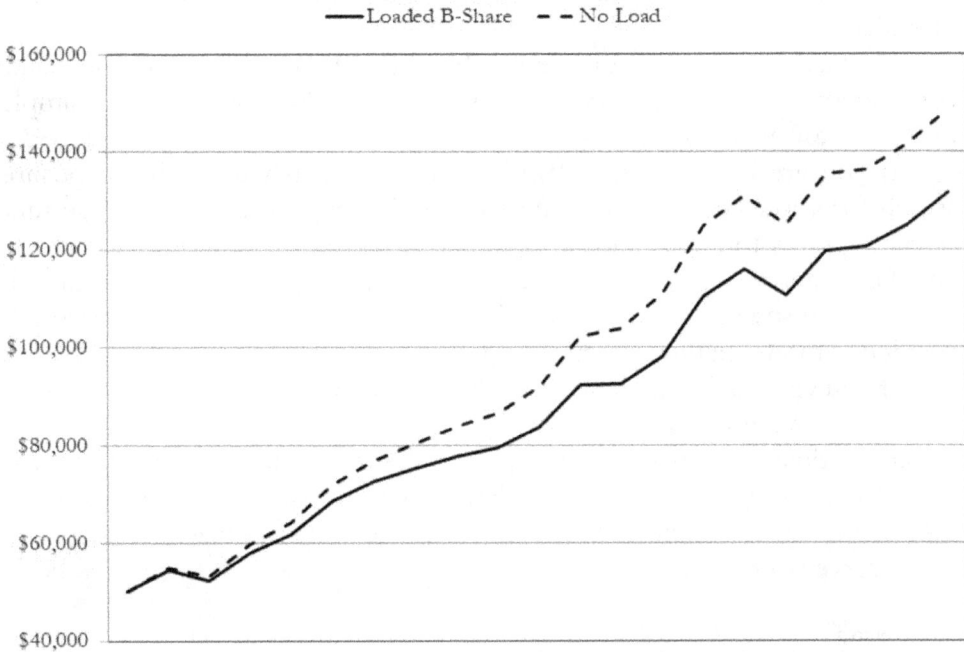

Back-end penalties

B-shares come with contingent back-end fees that hit if shares are sold during the first several years. This charge assures commissions for the sales team. These charges damage your wealth and create disincentives to moving money. There may be times you want to sell a particular investment. You may need cash for a large purchase or unexpected life change. Perhaps your risk profile shifts to a different asset allocation. Whatever your needs, you should always be able to access your own money. If you buy B-shares you will never recover all of it, and you will be disinclined to touch it at all, even for beneficial reasons.

Growing harm

As with A-shares, B-share fee damage worsens over time. Assuming a 1%, 7-year commission schedule and S&P 500 index returns, a $50,000 investment in a B-share stock fund from 1998 to 2017 would have forfeited over $13,000 in earnings obtainable with a no-load fund identically invested. An investment grade B-share bond fund would have sacrificed about 18% of the returns obtainable in a no-load equivalent during the same period.

What you should do instead

B-share funds are often the cornerstone of terrible retirement plans, such as corporate 401k plans. If you see B-share funds in your plan, speak with the person who determines your firm's benefits and request a change of providers.

If you're personally considering buying a B-share fund as the major component of your entire investment plan, read Section IV for a simple, proper investment regimen.

If you are considering a 'B' share fund to satisfy a specific exposure, search for a low-cost no-load fund with similar exposure. You can use fund screening tools found at Morningstar.com and good institutions like Schwab and TD Ameritrade. Minimize your expenses, perhaps with an index fund in the category sought. If your institution does not provide free access to low cost index funds, change institutions (Chapter 47).

If you've already purchased a B-share fund and are concerned about the back-end penalties, ignore the concern. The back-end penalties effective at any given time are usually about equal to the remaining commissions yet to be collected going forward. You're already contractually committed to paying the sales charges. Move forward now and get into no-load products that better serve your needs.

* Data sources:
Stock returns: S&P Dow Jones Indices LLC; Standard & Poor's 500 Index.
Bond returns: Federal Reserve Release H-15; An index of equal parts (25% each) Moody's Aaa corporate bonds, Moody's Baa corporate bonds, 5-year Treasury bonds, and 10-year Treasury bonds, rebalanced annually.
Fund expense rate: 0.2%
Loaded B-share sales charge: 1% per year for seven years.

27: Mutual Funds: Loaded C-Share Funds

What is a C-share mutual fund?

A C-share mutual fund is a class of fund with continuous sales charges instead of high upfront or back-end fees. Like B-shares, those sales charges result in a very high expense ratio. Unlike B-shares, those extra fees never end. Some C-shares also charge a front-end commission, but well below that of A-shares. Many C-shares also charge a back-end fee when shares are liquidated, but well below the back-end penalties B-shares can incur.

For years, reps found front-end loaded A-shares and back-end loaded B-shares hard to sell because of the obvious damage of the high fees. C-shares reduce the magnitude of those one-time charges while still allowing for the payment of commissions to the broker.

Figure 27-1: C-Share vs No-Load Stock Funds 1998-2017

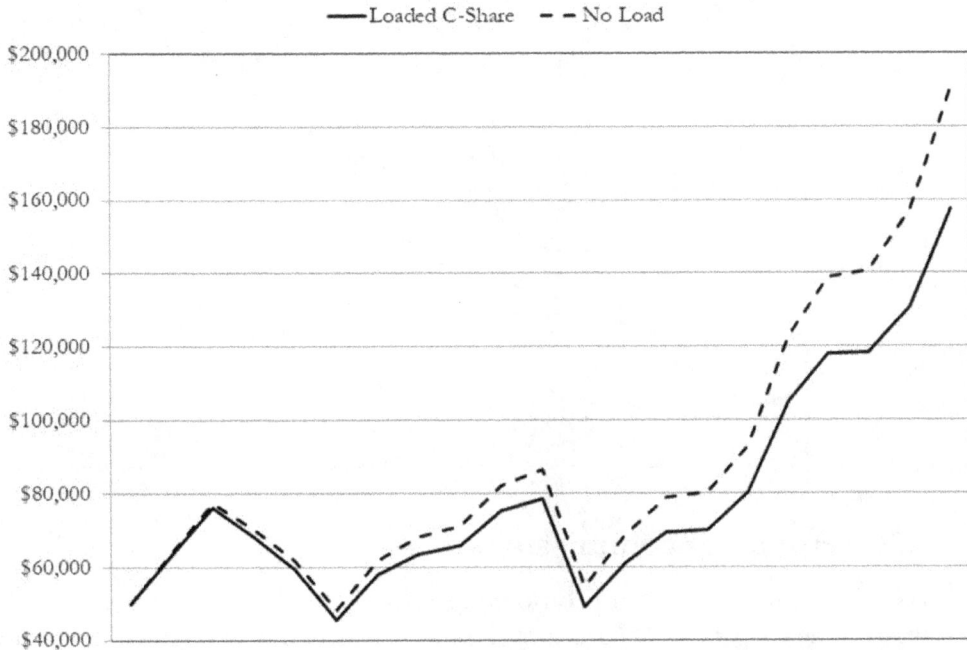

Why you should avoid C-share mutual funds

Continuous sales charges

Like other mutual funds, C-share funds incur management and administrative expenses. Continuous sales fees are added to these, resulting in high expense ratios, often 2% or more. This greatly damages potential growth, sometimes wiping out the entire yield of bonds and trimming average stock returns by 20-40%.

Transaction fees

The fees charged for purchasing and selling C-shares bleed assets upon every transaction. Though not as severe as the front and back-end charges of A- and B-shares, these fees create reticence to move money, making them harmful both in their direct cost and retardant impact on executing your desired strategy.

Figure 27-2: C-Share vs No-Load Bond Funds 1998-2017

─── Loaded C-Share   ─ ─ No Load

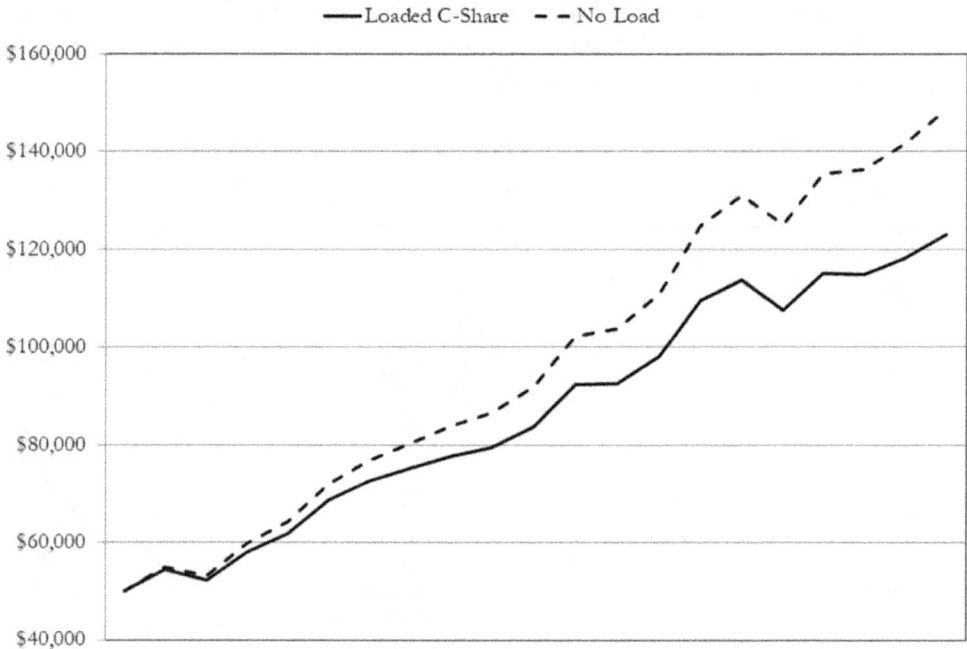

Never-ending commissions

C-share funds are often promoted as a low-cost alternative to A- and B-shares. In the long run, C-shares are the most destructive. The front-end load of A-shares hits only once. The annual sales fees tacked onto B-shares end after several years. C-share fees never end. Sometime between five and eight years C-share costs pass those of the other classes. A C-share fund tracking the S&P 500 with a 0.2% management fee and 1% annual sales commission from 1998 through 2017 would have grown a $50,000 investment to $157,429 (Figure 27-1). A no-load fund in the same stocks would have reached $190,613. This $33,184 forfeiture vastly exceeds the damage of both A- and B-shares.

What you should do instead

If you own or are considering a C-share fund for a specific exposure, find a low-cost no-load fund with similar focus. If the relevant C-share fund is your main investment read Section IV for a proper investment regimen. If you do not have free access to low cost no-load index funds at your institution, switch institutions (Chapter 47).

* Data sources:
Stock returns: S&P Dow Jones Indices LLC; Standard & Poor's 500 Index.
Bond returns: Federal Reserve Release H-15; An index of equal parts (25% each) Moody's Aaa corporate bonds, Moody's Baa corporate bonds, 5-year Treasury bonds, and 10-year Treasury bonds, rebalanced annually.
Fund expense rate: 0.2%. Loaded C-share sales charge: 1% annually.

28: Mutual Funds: Long/Short Funds

What is a long/short mutual fund?

When you own shares of a stock, in the vernacular of Wall Street you are "long" that stock. If you sell stock that you do not own – stated otherwise, you owe stock to someone – you are "short" that stock. On Wall Street, as a regular course of business, people are allowed to sell securities they do not yet own.

A long/short mutual fund is an investment company holding both long and short positions. Generally, these funds will be long (own) those things its managers like and short (owe) those things its managers don't like.

Mechanically, when you sell a security you receive cash. That cash can be invested. A common long/short structure is abbreviated 130/30. For every $100 received from fund investors like you, another $30 is raised through the short sale of supposedly bad things, providing $130 to invest in supposedly good things. The net value is still only $100, since $30 worth of sold securities is still owed – at least on day one.

In theory, the securities bought will go up by more than the sold ones, providing even better returns than a portfolio with only 100% invested in the "good stuff". In a best-case scenario, the bought stocks go up and the sold ones go down, allowing the manager to buy the sold ones back at a lower price and thus make profits on both sides of the trades.

Why you should avoid long/short funds

Poor performance of managed money

One of the selling points of long/short funds is the opportunity to magnify the benefits of excellent portfolio management. If a manager can do great things with all of your money, imagine what he or she could do for you with even more. Additionally, if you can profit from winners, why not profit from losers found with the very same system. The problem is reality: most professional money managers are beaten by the markets.

As discussed in Chapter 29, indices beat active mutual fund managers most of the time. Since an index is by definition average, active stock managers historically do a terrible job choosing winners and losers. Inferential evidence suggests you are better off owning stocks these managers want to sell and selling short the ones they want to buy.

Indeed, while $10,000 invested in an S&P 500 index fund would have grown to $22,344 during the decade ending 2017, the same amount earning the average return of all long/short mutual funds tracked by Morningstar would have grown to only $13,078. Versus the annualized rate of 8.37%

earned by the index fund over this period, long/short funds earned a paltry 2.72%.

Figure 28-1: Long/Short Funds vs Markets 2008-2017

──── Morningstar Long Short Fund Category Average

– – Vanguard 500 Index Fund

--- Vanguard Total Bond Market Index Fund

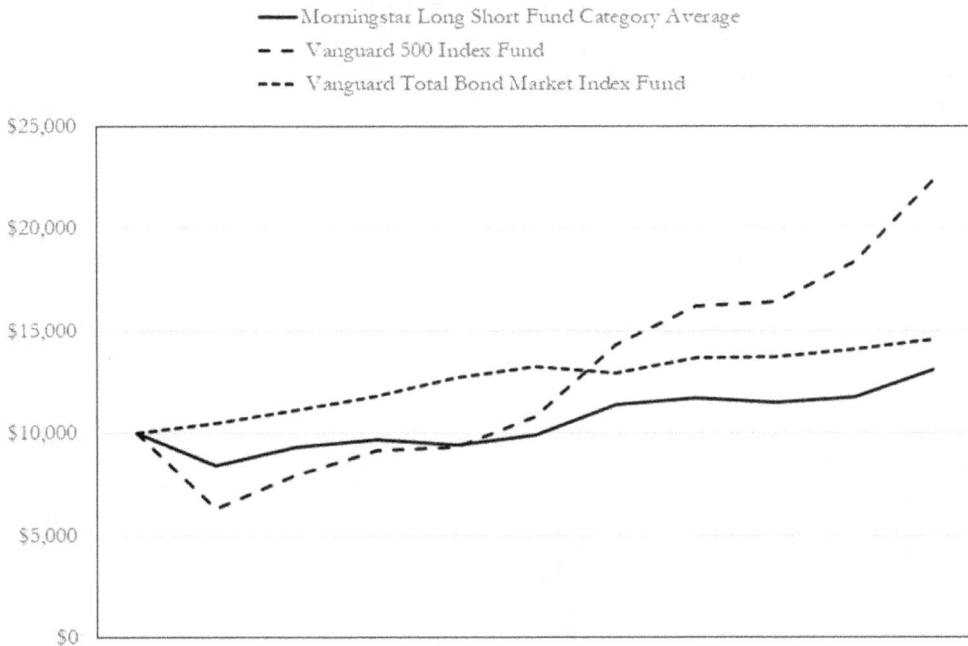

Greater uncertainty

With most funds, your exposure is limited to the amount of money you've invested. If you place $10,000 into a large-cap stock fund you will own at most $10,000 worth of large-cap stocks.

If you put $10,000 into a long/short fund, the net value at first will be $10,000 but your actual exposure could be far greater. Using the 130/30 model, you might own $13,000 worth of long positions and owe $3,000 worth of short positions. You would have $16,000 of exposure.

Stocks usually move in the same direction, so the $3,000 of short positions should offset about $3,000 of the long positions. But there are no guarantees. It is possible for the short stocks to go up, increasing what you owe while the long stocks go down. If the up and down movements were each 5%, this long/short fund would be down 8%.

The hope and intention of the fund design is the opposite. But the hope and intention of managed money in general is to beat the market. This does not happen much.

What you should do instead

Take long/short funds out of your consideration. If you already own shares, liquidate them. If you like the particular exposure such as large-cap value or small-cap growth, invest in a low-cost, no-load index mutual fund with that specific exposure. If the long/short fund was to be your primary investment vehicle, turn to Section IV for better direction.

* Data sources:
The Vanguard Group, Inc., Morningstar, Inc.

29: Mutual Funds: Managed Funds

What is a managed mutual fund?

A managed mutual fund is one in which a decision-making process determines security selection. While index funds seek to mimic the returns of a particular index such as the Standard & Poor's 500, a managed mutual fund sets different goals, like maximizing growth, generating high income or perhaps beating a specified index. The decisions can come from a single manager, a team or even a computer program.

There is nothing pernicious about the concept of having active fund management. The goals of most are usually sound. The managers and their staffs are likely very smart. Many no-load managed funds present appropriate diversification, logically structured portfolios and reasonable expense levels for the work being done. The problems with managed funds arise with market characteristics and human nature that have historically led to shareholder disappointment.

Why you should avoid managed mutual funds

Poor long-term results

Annually, about 65% of managed mutual funds underperform the indices they're attempting to beat. Over 10-year spans, that percentage sits around 80%, and over 20-year spans it hits 90%. Since you invest for the long run, you face a managed fund universe in which only one in ten outpaces the relevant funds in the indexed universe. Moreover, there is no way to correctly guess which few funds will be the winners. Multiple surveys confirm the poor performance of managed money. Figure 29-1 highlights a few.

Over-hyped short-term results

You will never see a mutual fund advertise how poorly it did, but you can easily find plenty of ads for funds that did well recently. Because of this skewed information flow, many people mistakenly believe professional money managers know how to beat the market. They do not.

There are thousands of financial professionals and millions of amateurs who buy and sell stocks and bonds every day using all information available. Their combined activity renders efficient prices. Fund managers buy securities with future expectations no greater than anything you might randomly buy.

Tendency toward indexing

If you decide to pay more for managed money, you expect something better than an index. However, many managed mutual funds have grown so large they have become closet index funds. Most funds have restrictions on the percentage of assets they can put into any one company. Forced to spread assets in every direction, these funds have expected returns similar to an index, minus fees.

Figure 29-1: Underperformance of Active Fund Management

Source	Period Covered	Percent of Active Funds Outpaced by Index Funds
White Paper: "A Case for Index Fund Portfolios", Ferri & Benke, for Betterment LLC, New York, 2013	1997-2012	82.90%
Study by NerdWallet Inc., San Francisco, 2013	2002-2012	76.00%
Standard & Poor's Indices Versus Active (SPIVA) Scorecard - Large Cap	2009-2013	72.72%
Standard & Poor's Indices Versus Active (SPIVA) Scorecard - Mid Cap	2009-2013	77.71%
Standard & Poor's Indices Versus Active (SPIVA) Scorecard - Small Cap	2009-2013	66.77%

High fees

Many index funds charge annual fees of less than a tenth of a percent. Most managed funds charge much more; many have fees in the 1.5% to 2.5% range. These rates are as damaging as they are sad given the poor results.

What you should do instead

If you own or are considering a managed mutual fund to fulfill a specific investing need, seek an index fund that invests in the same category.

If your managed fund ownership represents your primary investment involvement, read Section IV for a more effective regimen and detailed fund guidance.

30: Mutual Funds: Target Date Funds

What is a target date mutual fund?

A target date mutual fund is an asset allocation fund (Chapter 19) in which the allocation changes over time. The date cited in the fund name refers to the time of the event for which you are saving; usually retirement but theoretically any big ticket expense. For instance, if you expect to retire in 2040 or have a child starting college in 2040, you might seek a target date fund with 2040 in its name.

Using assumptions consistent with the oft-used but foolish strategy known as age-based asset allocation (Chapter 35), target date funds become increasingly conservative over time, shifting assets from stocks to bonds. For example, a fund 30 years from its target date might have 90% of its assets in stocks and 10% in bonds. A fund five years from its target date might have 30% of its assets in stocks and 70% in bonds.

Figure 30-1: Target Date Misallocation to Stocks

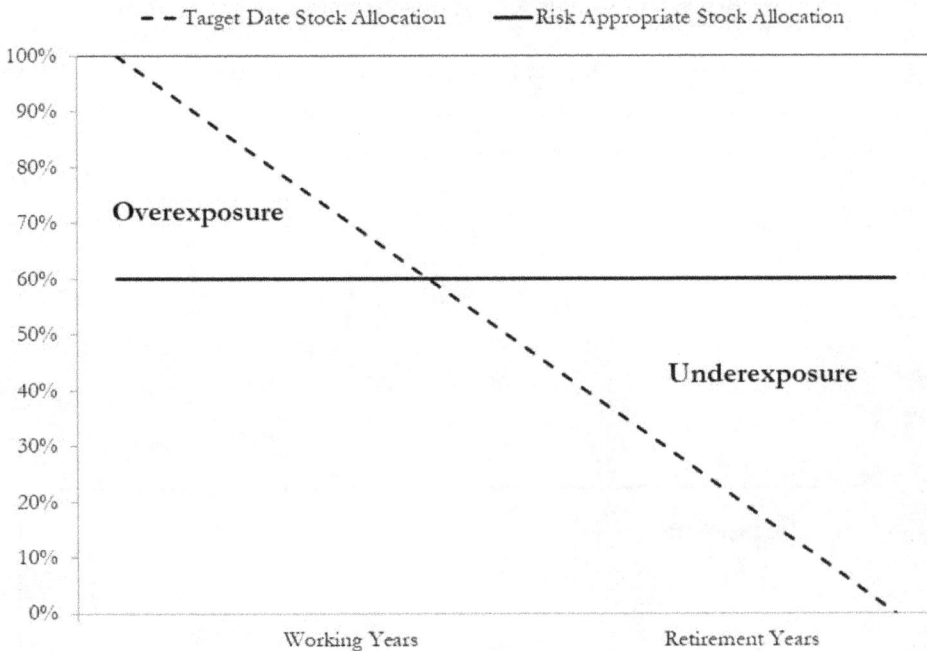

Why you should avoid target funds

Dependence on a flawed principle

The chief operating principle in the management of target date funds is the steady shift of assets from growth-oriented securities like stocks to conservative income instruments like bonds. This shift occurs regardless of market conditions.

More importantly, the asset allocation ignores your risk tolerance. There are timid young investors. There are aggressive return maximizers already in retirement. With target date funds, nervous young investors suffer unwanted volatility, while nervy seniors see their wealth prospects needlessly reduced.

Figures 30-1 and 30-2 plot an assumed risk-appropriate allocation of 60% stocks/40% bonds versus the allocations over time in a typical target date fund. Whatever your tolerance level, the mindless adjustment of assets in a target date fund will leave you perpetually over- or underexposed to each of the major asset categories.

High fees for service provided

Most target date funds include bonds in the asset mix. Bond portfolios usually require less intense management than stock portfolios, so bond mutual fund management fees are a fraction of the rate charged by stock mutual funds. Yet most target date funds have expense ratios appropriate for 100% stock portfolios; an annual overcharge that worsens with time.

Figure 30-2: Target Date Misallocation to Bonds

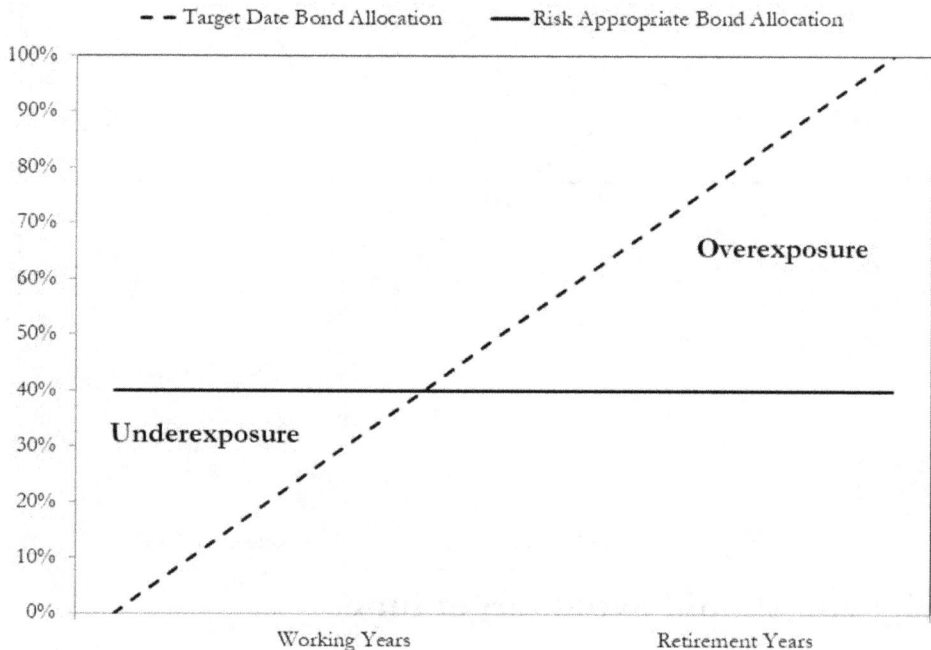

What you should do instead

First, do not use a calendar to determine the constituents of your portfolio. Ignore your birthday, your expected retirement date and any other date before or after. Since target date funds rely on a calendar for strategy, ignore them as well.

If you are already invested in or considering a target date fund as your holistic one-stop solution, the superior replacement strategy is a proper overall investment program. You can find such a program in Section IV. Chapters 45 and 46 within that section can help you determine your tolerance for risk and appropriate asset allocation target.

31: Mutual Fund Wrap Programs

What is a mutual fund wrap program?

A mutual fund wrap program is a platform through which investors pay fees to gain easy access to a plethora of mutual funds. Not to be confused with a mutual fund platform providing free access to thousands of funds, wrap programs tack on their own annual fees and highlight funds normally burdened by sales commissions.

Wrap programs are presented as a way to avoid these sales loads: You pay the annual charge of a percent or two on your entire balance while the broker exempts you from A-, B-, and C-share commissions.

Why you should avoid mutual fund wrap programs

Damaging fees

Mutual fund wrap programs were created to collect commissions while masking them. The funds they include already charge for portfolio management and administration. Wrap fees are an added expense collected and paid to salespeople.

Figure 31-1: Wrap Program Impact on Stock Funds 1998-2017

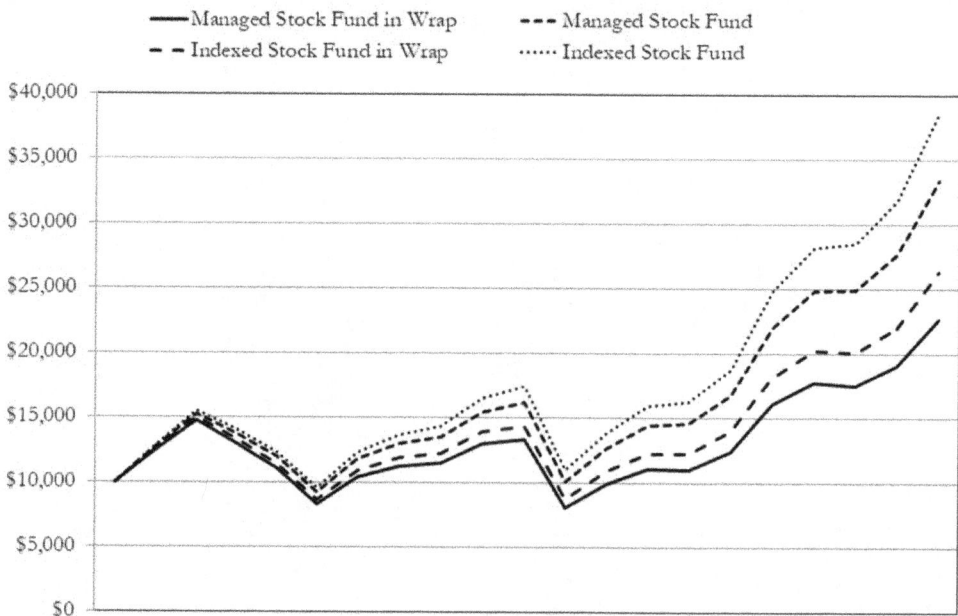

Fund wrap fee rates vary, often falling in the 0.5-2% range. Combining all expenses, a managed fund in a wrap program could cost well over 2-3%;

enough to wipe out the income of many bond funds and a substantial portion of stock returns.

Lack of service

Mutual funds are managed by portfolio managers and staff to whom fees are paid. Fund shares also incur administrative costs. Portfolio management and administration are actual services. The fees charged for access to a wrap program have nothing to do with service or benefit to you. They create revenues for salespeople.

Figure 31-2: Wrap Program Impact on Bond Funds 1998-2017

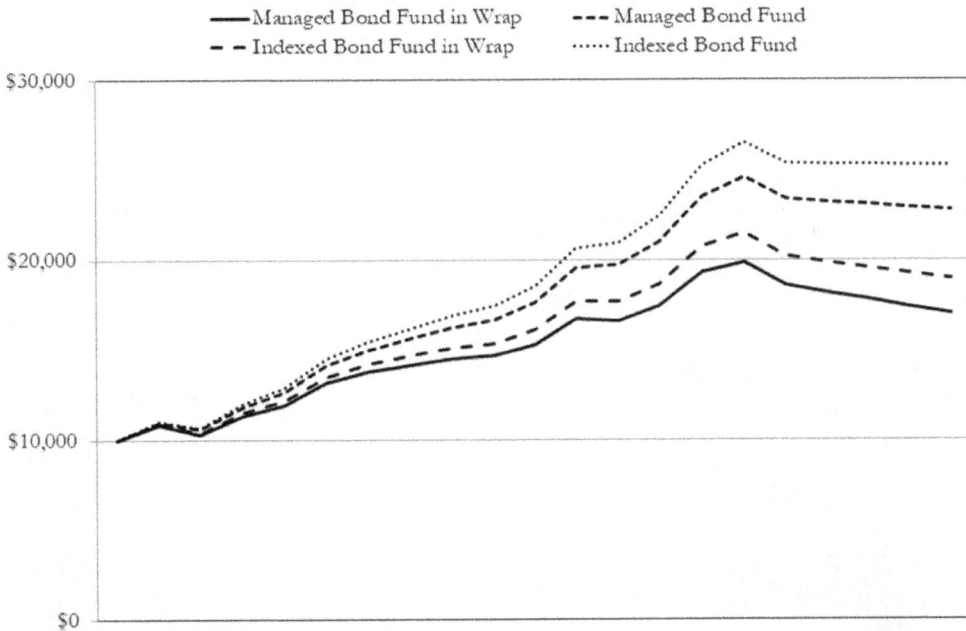

What you should do instead

If your investments are held at an institution with a fee-charging mutual fund wrap program, whether or not you participate in that program you should switch institutions. The wrap is most likely only one of many mechanisms they have in place to strip your assets. See Chapter 47 and Appendix A for help finding a better institution.

If you are not attached to your fund choices, this is a good time to reassess your regimen. Read Section IV for guidance.

* Data sources:
Stock returns: S&P Dow Jones Indices LLC; Standard & Poor's 500 Index.
Bond returns: Federal Reserve Release H-15; An index of equal parts (25% each) Moody's Aaa corporate bonds, Moody's Baa corporate bonds, 5-year Treasury bonds, and 10-year Treasury bonds, rebalanced annually.

Fund expense rates: Investment Company Institute averages - managed stock funds 0.89%, indexed stock funds 0.12%, managed bond funds 0.65%, indexed bond funds 0.11%.
Wrap account expense rates: stocks 2%, bonds 1.5%.

32: Options

What is an option?

An option is a contract between two investors wherein one pays money to the other in exchange for the right to buy or sell something at a given price before a set date. A call option grants the buyer the right to buy something. A put option grants the buyer the right to sell something. The money paid for the option is called the premium. The price specified in the option is called the strike price. The date through which the option exists is called the expiration date.

Options are often used to increase income, protect and speculate.

Income

A common income enhancing technique is selling "covered calls". For premium – money received – you can sell a call option on a stock held in your portfolio. If the stock price remains under the strike price until expiration, the premium you received is a pure gain for which you gave up nothing. Moreover, after the option expires, you could sell a new covered call on the very same stock with a new strike price and expiration date. This can go on and on.

Offsetting this extra income is your reduced potential gain. If the stock underlying the call goes above the strike price, the owner of the call will exercise the right to take the stock from you at the option strike price. Yet, if the stock goes down, as owner you experience all the loss.

Protection

There are times you will be nervous about near-term market prospects. You can sell stock and hope for good timing; a rare event (Chapter 42). You can weather the storm. Alternatively, you can buy put options for one or more of the stocks in your portfolio. If the price of a stock falls below the put strike price you will be able to exercise the put option and receive that strike price for your shares. If the stock price rises, you still own the stock and profit accordingly. Of course the money you spend on put options will be money out the door in either situation.

Speculation

Options can be used to profit from stock movements far more dramatically than you could through the stocks themselves.

For example, a 100-share lot of a $100 stock costs $10,000. If the stock price moves up $10, your profit would be $1,000, or 10%. If a call option on the same stock costs $10, you could buy options on 1,000 shares for the same $10,000 investment. Given the same $10 increase in the share price and a one-for-one increase in the option price, your options value will rise by $10,000, a 100% rate of return. Conversely, if the stock did not rise above the call price before the expiration date, the options would become worthless – a loss of 100%.

Why you should avoid options

Nothing is secured

Options are derivative securities. They are contracts that expire relatively quickly. Often there are no resulting transactions other than an option's creation and expiration.

Negative sum game

Bond market participants can all do well as interest is paid to all holders. Similarly, all stock market participants can do well in the long run as economic growth leads to earnings growth, share price gains and dividends. But for every option there is a winner and loser. At best, trading options is a zero-sum game. Because there are transaction costs, it is actually a negative sum game.

Total loss a frequent occurrence

Some fans of options trading suggest they are a mechanism to buy into a company cheaply. Why pay $100 for a stock when you can pay $5 for a call option? This is a false comparison. What matters with any investment is the upside potential versus downside risk. If you buy a stock and it goes down 5%, you still have 95% of your investment. If you buy a call option on a stock at its current price and the stock drops 5%, you will have lost every penny you spent. Further, if you sell options and the market goes in the opposite direction you were hoping, your potential losses are unlimited.

The dramatic impact of option behavior is demonstrated in the following charts. Both assume a current stock price of $100 and a $5 cost for a call option on the same stock with a strike price of $100. Figure 32-1 shows the dollar gain and loss per unit (share/option) given ending prices for the stock between $90 and $110. The stock investment has zero profit or loss if nothing changes; it gains and loses value dollar for dollar. The option generates a loss if nothing happens, if the stock goes down, or if the stock rises by less than the cost of the option. Once the stock is above $105, the option is profitable.

Figure 32-2 highlights the percentage returns as of the expiration of the option. In the case of the stock, a $1 decline renders a 1% loss; a $10 decline, a 10% loss. Rises by the same amounts generate profits of equivalent percentages. In the case of an option, if the stock falls at all, you lose 100% of your investment. If the stock does not move, you also lose everything. If the stock rises $1, the option "only" renders an 80% loss. If it goes up $2, the damage is 60% of your proceeds. If the stock gains $5, the cost of the option is recouped and you break even. Gains greater than $5 will finally create profit.

Figure 32-1: Options vs Stocks – Unit Gain/Loss

- - Stock ——Option

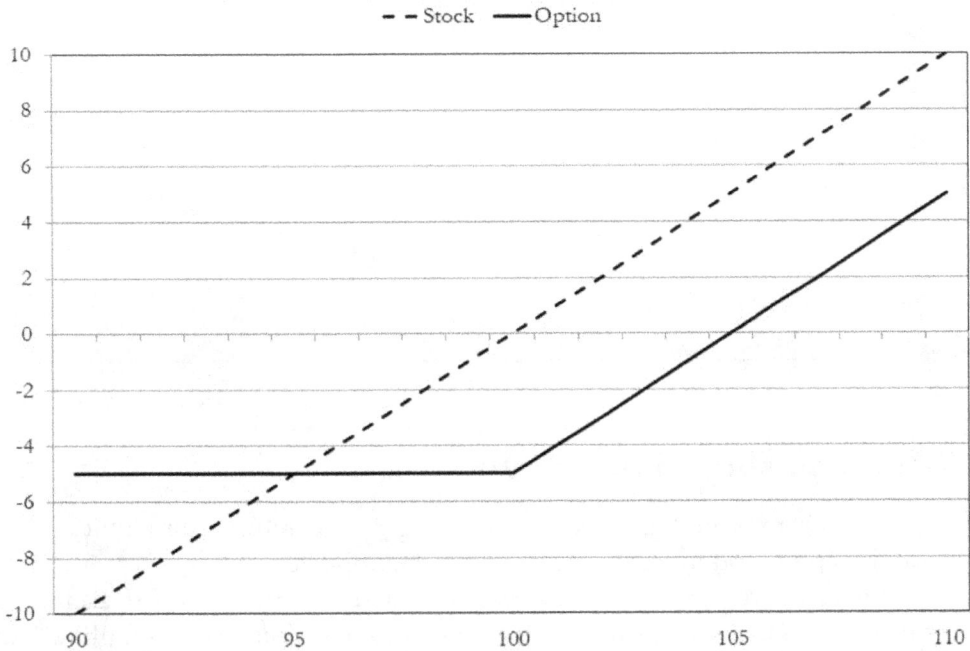

Options entail some possibility for gain; they would not exist otherwise. But instead of mild underperformance in the case of a wrong guess, bad timing or mere stability, options risk total loss.

Perpetual deterioration

Options have an expiration date. When you buy one, part – sometimes all – of the premium you pay is an extra amount that takes into account how much time remains for the conditions of the option to render profits. If a stock sells for $100, a call option that allows you to buy that stock at $95 will cost about $5 on the day it expires. But a $95 call option expiring in two months will cost much more than $5 because a lot can happen during that period. If you pay $12 for the option, $5 is 'intrinsic value' representing the difference between the stock price and the strike price; $7 is the time value. This time value will decline to nothing as of the expiration date. All options will lose all of their time value upon expiration.

Figure 32-2: Options vs Stocks – % Gain/Loss

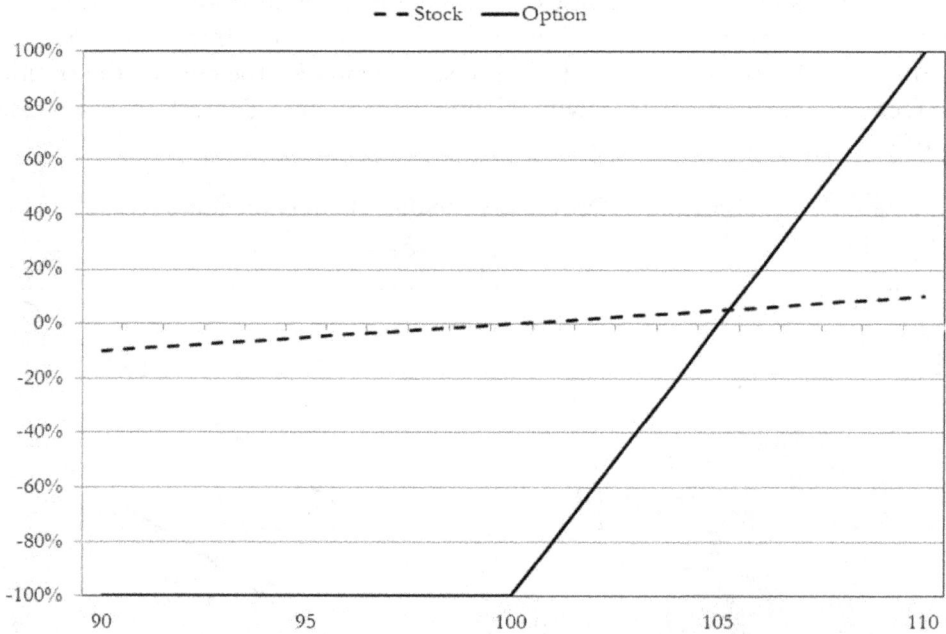

- - Stock ——Option

What you should do instead

Options present high risk, negative aggregate returns and much time commitment. Good investing emphasizes the opposite.

If your interest in buying call options is based on the hope for magnified returns from a stock you like, buy the stock instead. You could be right about the long-term prospects of a company, buy options, and still lose your entire investment upon expiration. Owning the stock you can be patient and profit.

If your interest in buying put options is based on fear of imminent loss of portfolio value, beware the folly of trying to time markets (Chapter 42). If the bad events you expect do not transpire before expiration, you face total loss on the options held and the hard choice of spending even more money for more puts. Instead, you could sell the stock you now hold in disfavor and either buy something else or hold cash for a spell.

If your interest in selling options is to generate extra income, skip it. The income from options represents the maximum you can gain. If the stock moves in the wrong direction, your potential losses – or lost opportunities for gain – are huge; many times the income you receive. Consider stocks and stock funds with higher than average dividends and bonds.

33: Private Placements

What is a private placement?

A privately placed security is one that does not get offered to the public when first issued. Private issues of stocks and bonds are usually offered to a limited number of large investors such as mutual funds and rich individuals.

Unlike public offerings of securities, private placements do not require the generation of a prospectus or registration with the SEC. Often these deals are disclosed after the transactions have taken place.

If you work for a private company and receive shares as compensation, wonderful. If you believe your firm has great promise and you are presented with the opportunity to buy a verifiable stake, it is something to consider. Ditto regarding firms for which you have intimate, substantiated information indicating great prospects. Otherwise, without intimate access to material corporate information and a high probability of positive outcome, it is prudent to stay away from private securities.

Why you should avoid private placements

Limited liquidity

When you own a private security, your choices for selling it are very limited. There is no obligation for anyone to buy it back from you. There are no exchanges for you to find a buyer, or even a price. Effectively, your sale would represent a private placement of its own. The odds that you will get a fair price are quite small. Even if bought back by the issuer or the investment banker who did the deal, they will factor in the costs of remarketing your stake in coming up with a price for you.

Lack of information

One reason deals are done privately is to avoid the bureaucratic process of filing with the SEC. Many of these filings provide information needed to analyze the value of a stock or credit worthiness of a bond. Without such, you are reliant on brochures from an investment banking salesperson or the firm wanting your money. Neither should be taken at their word.

Fraud likely, not just possible

Given the lack of filing requirements, private placements are a common vehicle for defrauding investors. SEC rules were established to protect the public. Many purveyors of private placements seek to evade these protections, not the bureaucracy. Information provided need not be audited or confirmed by an independent third party. Put another way, the person coming privately to you for money was either rejected by, or did not even approach, bankers, venture capitalists and other professional financiers. Sound suspicious?

What you should do instead

Aside from firms for which you have intimate and substantiated information, stay away from private securities. If you receive a call or email regarding an opportunity to own a stake in an oil field, or a chance to be involved with film production, or a new medicine, or real estate, or any private investment whatsoever, ask to be put on their "do not call" list. Then hang up. All securities mentioned in Section IV and Appendix B are public.

34: Real Estate (Beyond Your Home)

What is real estate?

We're familiar with houses, condominiums and other abodes as living options. As investments, you can buy other properties same as you'd buy a home, with deeds, mortgages, closing costs; the whole nine yards. You can also invest in real estate investment trusts (REITs), mutual funds, closed end funds and exchange traded funds focused in real estate. Some of these funds emphasize income, seeking malls and other complexes with paying lessees. Other funds aim for total return, seeking undervalued properties.

Broad index funds will have some exposure to real estate, as they do all industries. You can keep your investment process simple, invest in index funds and accept whatever their sector weights are.

If you are not a homeowner, you might view devoted real estate exposure as a way to keep some assets tuned to property prices. A fund screener at your discount broker or Morningstar.com can help you develop a list of real estate investments. Choose low expense, no-load products. Check the properties owned by the funds under consideration to ensure geographic diversification. Real estate is a notoriously local business; you do not want to share the pains of an unfortunate region.

If you are a homeowner, consider ruling this sector out.

Figure 34-1: Average Household Real Estate Exposure

	With no Retirement Assets	With Retirement Assets
Cash	4,100	4,100
Taxable Investments	17,100	17,100
Retirement Plan		59,000
Total Financial Assets	21,200	80,200
Home	170,000	170,000
Total Investable Assets	191,200	250,200
Real Estate "Exposure"	89%	68%
Cash	2%	2%
All Other Investments	9%	30%

Why you should avoid real estate if you own a home

Homeowners are already heavily exposed to the real estate market. As reported in the September 2014 Federal Reserve Bulletin reviewing family finances, the median home price in the U.S. in 2013 was about $170,000. Meanwhile the median level of financial assets of any kind was $21,200. Less than half the households surveyed have retirement accounts; the median balance of these was $59,000. Disturbingly, more than half have no retirement related accounts at all.

Clearly, your house is an important investment. Citing the national figures above, a home represents between 68% and 89% of an average family's total investable assets. You may be among the lucky who are well above the median in terms of wealth and savings; if so, your home is probably well above the median value as well. The key here is recognition of your home as part of your portfolio. Owning a home and then buying more real estate for investment purposes is like a corn farmer buying more corn after a successful harvest.

What you should do instead

Estimate the value of your home (or homes). Add up the value of all of your other investments. Combine these two numbers for a grand total. Divide the home value into the grand total to obtain the percent of your assets already invested in real estate.

If this percentage is under 20%, you have room to consider other real estate investments. You certainly have no obligation.

If the percentage is over 20%, you already have more than adequate exposure. Avoid REITs and funds concentrated in real estate. Consider selling any you own and deploy the proceeds in a manner consistent with your overall investment regimen. If you have yet to develop a proper regimen, refer to Section IV for guidance.

* Data source:
Federal Reserve Bulletin Volume 100, Number 4, September 2014; Survey of Consumer Finances

Section III

Tactics You Should Avoid

35: Age-Based Asset Allocation

What is age-based asset allocation?

Age-based asset allocation is an investment strategy in which your age determines your mix of stocks and bonds. When approaching and then entering retirement, you will supposedly need more income to offset lost wages and less future growth since you will have, well, less of a future.

While formulas vary, a typical age-based asset allocation might have you subtract your age from 100. That number gives you the percentage you should invest in stocks; the rest would go into bonds. For instance, if you are 30 years old, you'd put 70% of your money in stocks, 30% in bonds. If you are 80, put 20% in stocks and 80% in bonds. This sounds simple and perhaps logical. It certainly is simple. It is also ignorant and irresponsible.

Figure 35-1: Age-Based Allocation Example

⊞ Stocks ⊟ Bonds

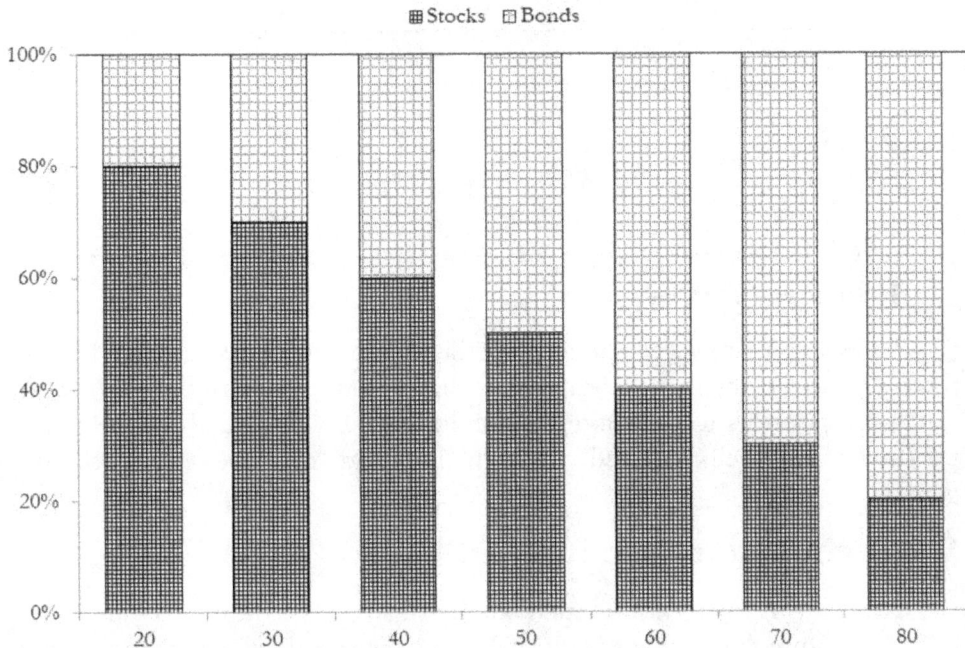

Why you should avoid age-based asset allocation

It ignores risk tolerance

There are nervous thirty-year-olds who would not be comfortable with most of their money in stocks. There are eighty-year-olds who want maximum asset growth. Age-based asset allocation ignores a basic precept of proper investing: maximize return at a level of risk appropriate to the individual. Most large financial firms provide detailed questionnaires to their reps to help them determine client risk profile. It's a foolish rep who ignores these questionnaires to rely on client birthdays.

It ignores demographics

Life expectancy grows as you age. If you reach age 60, it is likely you will live beyond 80. At 70, you will probably make it past 85. The average investment cycle, a period of time over which stocks and bonds typically go through bull and bear cycles to attain their long-term rates of return, is around seven years. So even at 70 you'll likely experience at least two complete investment cycles. Unless you have an extraordinarily conservative risk profile, you'd be foolish to hinder decades of returns with a portfolio excessively weighted in bonds.

Figure 35-2: Life Expectancy as of Attained Ages

Age Now	Remaining Years	Age Now	Remaining Years	Age Now	Remaining Years
0	77.8	35	44.6	70	15.2
5	73.5	40	39.9	75	12
10	68.5	45	35.3	80	9.2
15	63.6	50	30.9	85	6.8
20	58.8	55	26.7	90	5
25	54.1	60	22.6	95	3.6
30	49.3	65	18.7	100	2.6

It ignores family

Unless you expect to spend every last penny and pass nothing to heirs, their life expectancy is more important than yours. In wealthy families, elders don't dump stocks to generate income and stability. Handled correctly, their portfolios are well-managed through life and the lives of succeeding generations.

What you should do instead

Invest with logic, not a calendar. Ignore your birthday. Do not ignore bills. Make sure you have enough cash to cover your likely expenses over the next few months.

As for the rest, allocate assets among stocks and bonds in accordance with your tolerance for risk. Read Section IV for a proper regimen, including help in estimating your tolerance for risk (Chapter 45) as it pertains to asset allocation (Chapter 46).

* Data source:
U.S. Department of Health & Human Services; National Center for Health Statistics

36: Back-Testing

What is back-testing?

Back-testing is an analytical process in which historical data is used to determine the success or failure of a strategy. If a tested strategy generated good past results, one assumes it will do well in the future.

For example, you might believe dividend paying stocks perform better than stocks with no dividends. With a back-testing application, you can pretend you built a portfolio of dividend paying stocks ten years ago and then analyze how it performed in the ensuing decade. With good results, you might start shifting your assets into stocks with dividends or funds containing same. If the results are bad or neutral, you test other strategies until you find one with satisfactory returns.

Why you should avoid back testing

Past performance is irrelevant

Looking backward, you can "discover" all sorts of successful strategies. Unfortunately, you are not really finding anything of relevance. Very few stocks and sectors perform exactly in line with the market. By definition, some will be above average, others below. There are an infinite number of ways to group stocks. Some of those groupings will have performed better than others. Because they have done so in the past does not mean they will do so in the future. Consider the relative performance of the asset categories shown in Figure 36-1.

Each major asset category has its believers. Some investors favor growth, others value. Some like the 'action' in small-caps; others prefer the solid nature of large-caps. Some believe the best opportunities are found abroad. As Figure 36-1 demonstrates, no one major asset category has been consistently atop or beneath all the others. This lack of consistency among categories applies as well to groupings based on other factors such as yield, key ratios and industry.

Computers are back-testing 24/7

While you are reading this, computers throughout the world are running programs seeking patterns in a quest for excess profits. They analyze every publicly available statistic such as stock prices, corporate earnings and economic data. In the time it takes you to create a single strategy and run a back-test on a popular website, hundreds of computers have run millions of simulations. If there is value to any discernible statistical trait, multiple firms have already executed the trades and removed the opportunity before you've read your own test results and had your 'aha' moment.

Figure 36-1: Annual Asset Category Performance Ranking

2008	2009	2010	2011	2012	2013	2014	2015	2016	2017
Bonds 5.24%	Small Growth 34.47%	Small Growth 29.09%	Bonds 7.92%	Small Value 18.05%	Small Growth 43.30%	Large Growth 14.89%	Large Growth 5.52%	Small Value 31.74%	Large Growth 27.44%
Small Value -28.92%	Large Growth 30.77%	Small Value 24.50%	Large Growth 2.81%	Large Value 14.67%	Small Value 34.52%	Large Value 12.36%	Bonds 0.55%	Large Value 17.40%	Small Growth 22.17%
Small Growth -38.54%	Foreign 26.97%	Large Growth 13.18%	Large Value -2.87%	Small Growth 14.59%	Large Growth 32.75%	Bonds 5.97%	Small Growth -1.38%	Small Growth 11.32%	Foreign 21.78%
Large Growth -38.99%	Small Value 20.58%	Large Value 12.41%	Small Growth -2.91%	Foreign 13.55%	Large Value 31.99%	Small Growth 5.60%	Large Value -3.13%	Large Growth 6.89%	Large Value 15.36%
Foreign -43.38%	Large Value 16.54%	Bonds 6.54%	Small Value -5.50%	Large Growth 12.35%	Foreign 19.43%	Small Value 4.22%	Foreign -3.30%	Bonds 2.65%	Small Value 7.84%
Large Value -47.87%	Bonds 5.93%	Foreign 4.90%	Foreign -14.82%	Bonds 4.32%	Bonds -2.02%	Foreign -7.35%	Small Value -7.47%	Foreign -1.88%	Bonds 3.54%

Active management is of questionable merit

Even before computers came onto the scene in a big way, research revealed the futility of active equity management. Burton Malkiel's "A Random Walk down Wall Street (W.W. Norton & Company, Inc., 1973, reprinted many times since) popularized this notion while mutual fund data before and since have basically proven it.

With so many profit-seeking investors having access to the same public information, foreseeable excess gains are few, fleeting and rapidly eliminated. With current technology, reaction time to new information is measured in milliseconds. Over twenty-year periods, about 90% of actively managed mutual funds are outpaced by market indexes. When you back-test to make investment decisions, you are actively managing your money with vastly fewer tools than the pros who themselves consistently lag those same indices.

What you should do instead

Back-testing takes time and adds no value. If you have used it and profited, count yourself lucky and quit the game while you're ahead.

Look forward with your investments, not backward. Monday morning quarterbacking is as futile in investing as it is in football. Save time, avoid frustration and ignore back-testing tools. Invest with a logical, forward looking regimen such as outlined in Section IV.

* Data sources:
Small-cap value: Russell 2000 Value Index
Small-cap growth: Russell 2000 Growth Index
Large-cap value: Standard & Poor's / Barra 500 Value Index
Large-cap growth: Standard & Poor's / Barra 500 Growth Index
Foreign: Morgan Stanley Capital International EAFE Index
Bonds: Lehman Brothers Aggregate Bond Index

37: Chasing Winners

What is meant by "chasing winners"?

Chasing winners means buying securities with good recent performance. If a company's stock price rose of late, you might believe demand for its products will continue to rise. If a mutual fund has outperformed its peers, you might conclude it has more adept managers.

Why you should avoid chasing winners

Past is not prologue

Advertisements for investment firms include the caveat "past performance is not indicative of future results" or a similar phrase whenever citing returns. The law requiring this disclaimer exists because the disclaimer is true: past performance of a security provides zero clues on what will happen in the future.

Figure 37-1: 'Top Half' Funds Still Atop Next Year

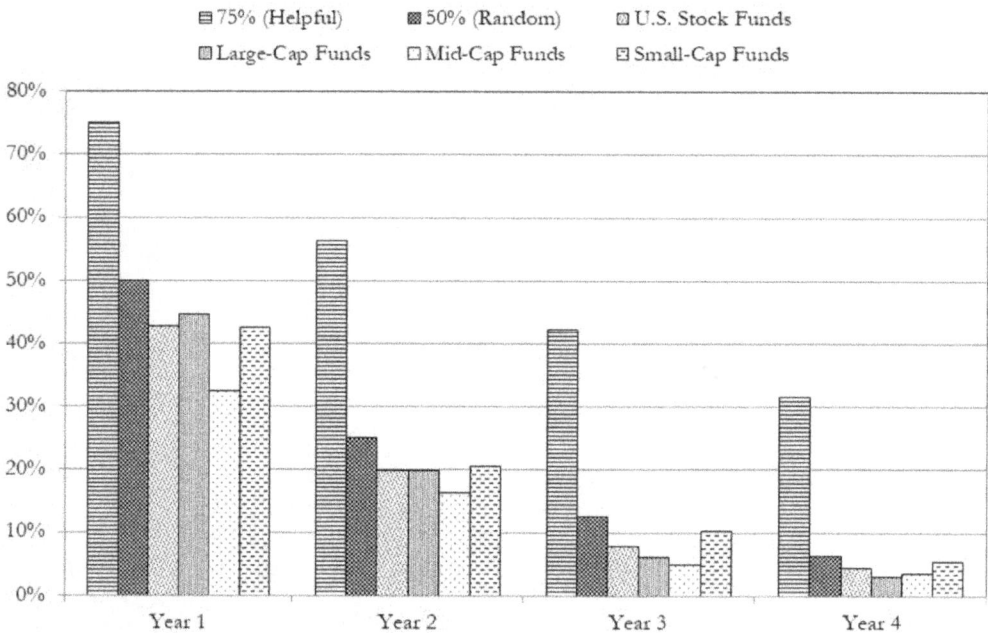

Legend:
- 75% (Helpful)
- 50% (Random)
- U.S. Stock Funds
- Large-Cap Funds
- Mid-Cap Funds
- Small-Cap Funds

Winners and losers often switch

In a recent study, Morningstar investigated relative returns of mutual funds. Within each investment category, funds were ranked according to performance each calendar year and split into two groups, top half and bottom half. Over time, Morningstar found funds in the bottom half one year were more likely to be in the top half the following year than those which had been in top half the first year. Those in the top half any given year were more likely to be in the bottom half the next year.

To further demonstrate the futility of choosing recent winners, Figure 37-1 graphs data from Standard & Poor's Persistence Scorecard, a survey in which all managed generic U.S. stock funds are tracked. First, S&P identified the top 50% of funds in terms of performance for the 12-month period ending March 31, 2010. Moving forward, S&P determined the percentage of these funds still in the top half for the following 12 months (ending March 31, 2011), the next 12 months (ending March 31, 2012) and onward. In the graph, each cluster of bars shows the percentage of 'top' funds still in the top half one, two, three, and four years later. If choosing winners is helpful, way more than 50% of these top funds should still be in the top half year one. Going forward more than 50% of those remaining (ergo more than 50% of 50%, or 25%) should be in the top half year two, etc.

In the graph, the first bar in each cluster marks a 75% theoretical success rate, indicating outperformance. The second bar of each cluster marks the 50% success rate which would indicate irrelevance of picking winners. The four bars to the right in each cluster show, respectively, actual results of all top funds, top large-cap funds, top mid-cap funds and top small-cap funds.

The results are actually worse than random. Only 42.8% of the "best" funds as of the beginning of the study were in the top half as of the end of year one. Only 19.9% of the original group made the top half in year two; 25% would have indicated randomness. Just 7.9% were atop year three; versus 12.5% for mere irrelevance. 4.5% remained in the top half in year four, with 6.25% representing the random indicator. Not only did picking winners not help; it hurt.

Analytically, things change. Hype calms down. New becomes old and mistakes get corrected. If a company is ridiculously profitable, new firms enter their line of work. If a company struggles but survives, its stock price will probably reach a level from where it can grow like any other.

What you should do instead

Chasing winners is pointless. But don't infer a false conclusion: chasing losers is equally pointless. Win or lose, past behaviors do not indicate future results. Many bad firms fail, and many funds do poorly over long spells, especially those with high fees that damage returns year after year.

Indeed, 'winning' in investments is a relative term. Over 20-year spans, index funds have outpaced about 90% of the funds actively managed by professional money managers. That is a pretty high winning percentage. If you've banked on winners in the past, consider index funds for the future. If you seek an effective path, read Section IV.

* Data source:
S&P Dow Jones Indices LLC; S&P Persistence Scorecard, June 2014

38: Using Gold as a Safe Haven

What is gold (really)?

You've probably seen or heard commercials hawking gold as if it is better or safer than money. It is not.

In the distant past, gold had special importance when it was a universal medium of exchange and later served as a tool to stabilize exchange rates and thus the world economy. During financial crises, such as the stagflation episode in the late 1970s and the banking collapse in 2008, many investors rush to gold in kneejerk fashion. Some are opportunistic early buyers who foresee the panic. Most are naïve victims who buy gold after it has spiked well above its innate value.

Gold is just a metal, a mere commodity. It is comparable to wheat, oil, zinc, and pork bellies. Its price, in the long run, is most impacted by the demand for jewelry. It is not, nor will it become a currency. It will never replace cash.

Why you should avoid gold as a safe haven

It generates poor long-term returns

Over the years, gold has provided a rate of return worse than stocks and bonds. It has spiked up during times of panic, only to fall right back down thereafter. The closest indicator of a long-term trend for gold is the size of the global middle class. The economic rise of China and India had much to do with gold's performance in the early 2000s. Even including that spurt, though, equities and fixed income instruments have beaten it.

It is not an investment

Like other commodities (Chapter 11), gold is not really an investment. It rises and falls in reaction to supply and demand. Unlike stocks, which can grow through profitable operations, and bonds, which provide income, gold has no intrinsic quality through which you should expect some form of secular or steady performance.

It is volatile with episodes of massive loss

In finance, a safe haven should protect value. In bad financial times, a safe haven should be stable and liquid. When times are good, a safe haven may not have much upside but it should still be safe. In the early 1980s, when fears of hyperinflation ebbed, gold lost over half its value. More recently, once the crisis following the 2008 financial meltdown calmed, gold plummeted about 40%. These losses are worse than most stock market crashes. Over the past 50 years, gold has been almost twice as volatile as stocks and four times more volatile than bonds. Sure, gold rose dramatically as often as it fell. But this is the behavior of a speculative instrument – not a safe haven.

Figure 38-1: Gold vs Stocks, Bonds, Cash 1973-2017

– – Stocks   – – – Bonds   ⋯⋯ Cash   ——Gold

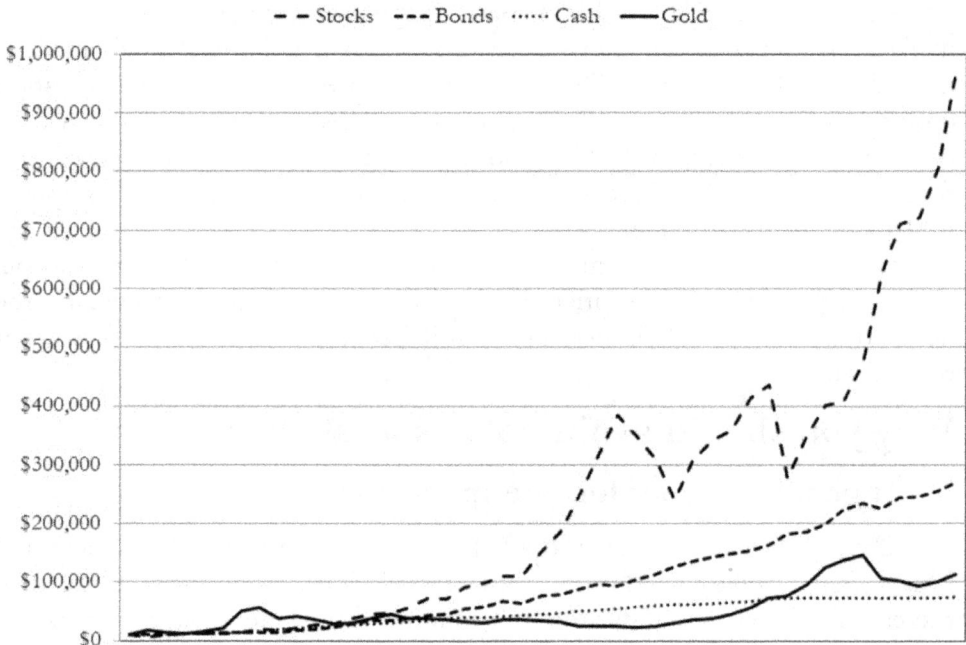

What you should do instead

If you define safety as 'absolute avoidance of loss,' you should seek protection in federally insured CDs, government bonds and/or money market funds. If you define safety as real after-inflation value in the long run, invest in stocks and bonds. Both provide better returns than gold with far less volatility. With lower returns and greater uncertainty, gold is the exact opposite of what a safe haven and investment in general should be.

* Data sources:
Stock returns: S&P Dow Jones Indices LLC; Standard & Poor's 500 Index.
Bond returns: Federal Reserve Release H-15; An index of equal parts (25% each) Moody's Aaa corporate bonds, Moody's Baa corporate bonds, 5-year Treasury bonds, and 10-year Treasury bonds, rebalanced annually.
Cash returns: 3-month Treasury bill rates
Gold prices: COMEX – Commodity Exchange Inc., New York Mercantile exchange since 1994.

39: Reading Charts

What is chart reading?

Chart reading is a form of analysis seeking patterns in security price movements. The relevant charts display price levels over time. Sometimes these charts will include moving averages. For example, today's 50-day moving average for stock X would be the average price of stock X over the past 50-days; yesterday's 50-day moving average would be the average from yesterday on back to the 50th day prior.

Certain features or patterns supposedly predict the future. A "head and shoulders" pattern, featuring a peak surrounded by two level plateaus, hints at near-term collapse. When a stock price crosses its 50-day moving average, a big move in the same direction might be imminent. Double tops and bottoms theoretically signify peaks and troughs.

Figure 39-1: SP 500 Index Daily Levels 2006-2013

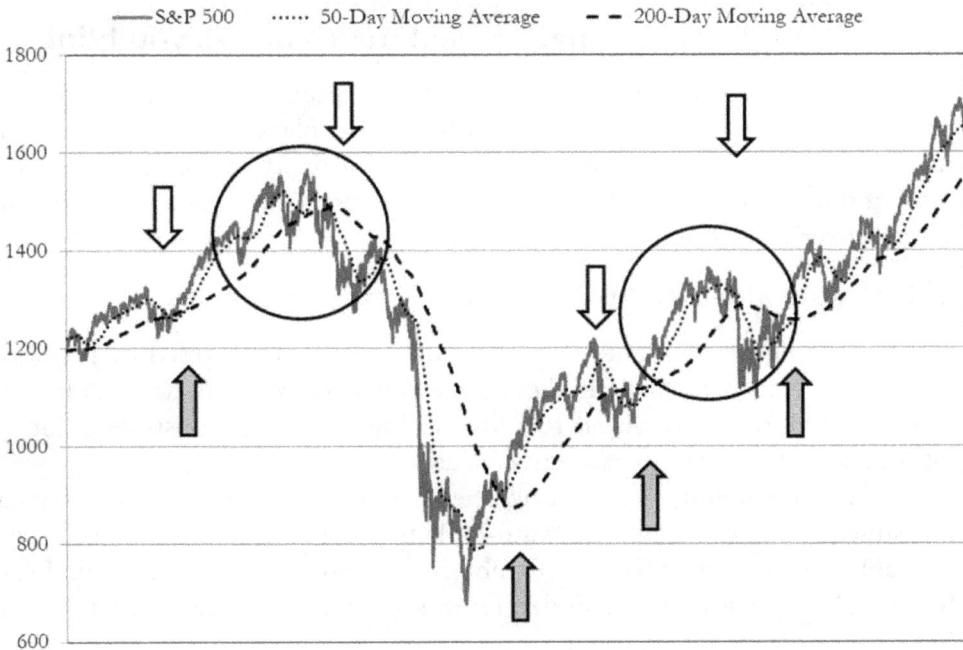

Figure 39-1 plots daily closing levels of the Standard & Poor's 500 over a 7-year span. Also shown are the course of the S&P 500's 50-day and 200-day moving averages. Circles mark a double and triple top. Arrows point to moments of theoretically important line crossings. On a live computer screen these charts look awesome. Some brokers promote their chart analyzing capabilities, citing "pattern recognition" tools as a snazzy, sophisticated benefit within their platforms. Snazzy they are; sophisticated and of benefit they are not.

Why you should avoid reading charts

Past movements indicate nothing

The price of any stock today reflects all publicly known information as of today. If the price of a stock changes tomorrow, it will be due to events or information not known today. It will have nothing to do with the price of the stock yesterday, the price fifty days earlier, or the pattern drawn by connecting the dots of those prices.

For instance, in Figure 39-1 you can spot as many head and shoulders patterns as you want depending on how wide the "head" and "shoulders". There is no predictable price movement after any of them. If you sold after the "double top" circled in 2008, you saved much; if you sold after the "triple top" in 2011 you lost much. As for the line crossings marked, more was lost than gained should you have traded according to the signals.

Computers will do math-based trades before you blink

As you read this, thousands of computer programs are analyzing the price patterns of every tradable security on the planet, seeking predictive relationships or improper pricing for possible profit. If any opportunities do present themselves, they will be long gone before you've read a report or run some broker's software.

What you should do instead

Discerning future market behavior based on shapes formed by previous prices has as much merit as predicting the course of your life with tea leaves. While charts are handy visual tools providing a quick synopsis of a lot of information, they have no predictive value.

When you invest, always look ahead. If chart reading is one of your investment tools, drop this backward-looking process. You will save time and probably avoid some misfires. Establish a healthy regimen instead. Read Section IV to save time, maximize returns for the risk accepted, and move forward.

* Data source:
S&P Dow Jones Indices LLC; Standard & Poor's 500 Index

40: Selling Short

What is selling short

Selling short means selling something you do not yet own. If you have a margin account at a brokerage, you have this capability.

For instance, if you felt the stock of company X was likely to drop, and you did not own it, you could still sell it at the current price. Your brokerage firm would borrow shares on your behalf, send them to the buying party and put money from the sale into your account. You can use that cash as if you deposited it yourself; it is a real asset.

However, you now also have a real liability as you owe shares of company X stock. To eliminate this liability, at some point in the future you must buy the same number of shares of company X stock. Upon purchase, you will have profited if the price is lower than when you sold it.

Why you should not sell short

Against historic price trend

In general, the stock market rises as the population grows and the economy expands. The Standard & Poor's 500, an index based on the stock price of 500 of the largest publicly traded corporations, crossed the 100 mark in 1968, 250 in 1986, 500 in 1995, 1000 in 1998, 1500 in 2007, 2000 in 2014, and 2500 in 2017.

In Figure 40-1, you can see how $1,000 invested in stocks grew during each 20-year span from 1938 to 2017. The worst of these 20-year periods saw gains of nearly 400%. Taking on positions that profit only when the market drops has historically been a losing proposition.

Market timing does not work

Though the market generally rises, downdrafts do occur. Unfortunately, declines are usually quick, dramatic, and unpredictable. Since selling short is a definite loser over long spells, it can only be viewed as a short-term, market timing mechanism. As demonstrated in Chapter 42, trying to time markets is foolish and potentially devastating to returns.

Unlimited potential loss

When you take a short position, your potential loss is theoretically infinite. After you have sold something for a set price, you have already received all potential proceeds. Going forward, if the stock price goes up, you will have to spend more money to buy it than you received selling it. If the stock doubles, you will spend twice as much and experience a loss equal to 100% of your original sale. If the stock triples, you will have to pay three times your original proceeds; and so on.

Figure 40-1: S&P 500 Returns over 20-Year Spans

——— 1998-2017 ⋯⋯ 1978-1997 – – 1958-1977 --- 1938-1957

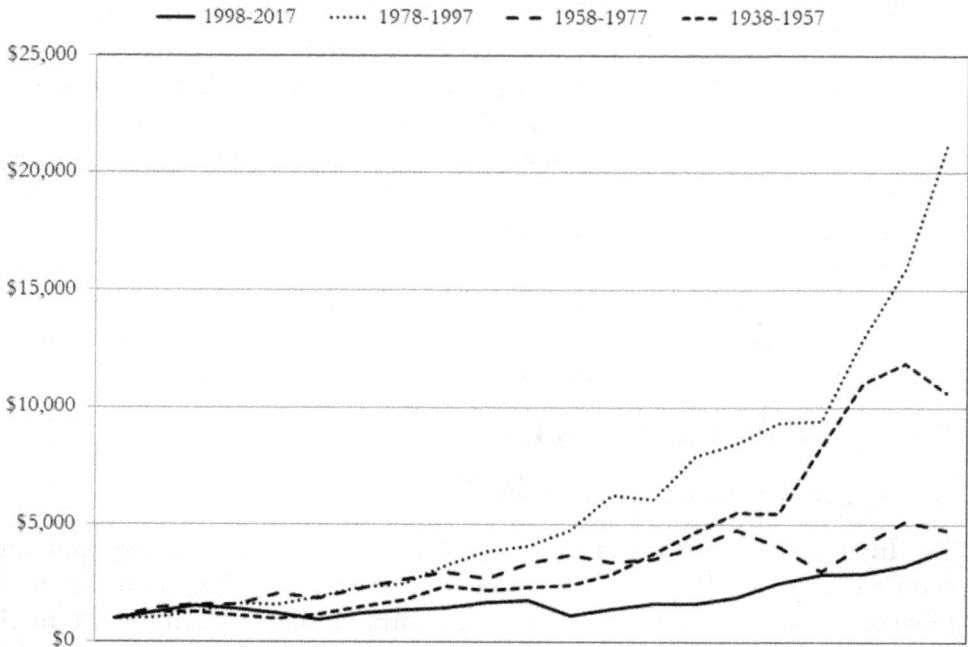

What you should do instead

If your temptation to sell short is a matter of trying to time the market, ignore the urge and stay invested at the level appropriate to your risk tolerance.

If your desire to sell short is due to a new level of concern, adjust your asset allocation instead. Do not take on a bad position, ever. Replace good volatile securities (stocks) with good stable securities (bonds, cash). When your concern abates and your tolerance for risk returns to its normal level, switch your holdings back.

* Data source:
S&P Dow Jones Indices LLC; Standard & Poor's 500 Index

41: Socially Responsible Investing

What is socially responsible investing?

Socially responsible investing is the attempt to limit portfolio holdings to firms whose operations are consistent with your sense of social propriety. You may want to deny money to the tobacco industry, utilities with nuclear power plants, perhaps food processors utilizing genetically modified products. Egregious polluters might be verboten. A socially responsible strategy seeks to maximize returns with securities still available after irresponsible firms are eliminated from consideration.

You can invest in socially responsible mutual funds and/or exchange traded funds. You can also develop your own portfolio of acceptable individual stocks. With so many thousands of companies to choose from, keeping sin out should not be too difficult, right?

Why you should avoid socially responsible investing

Limitations retard performance

Good investing is a process seeking maximal returns at an appropriate level of risk. Whenever you apply an artificial barrier, you hinder your ability to achieve those returns. In practice, socially responsible funds have performed worse than their unhindered peers. This is true of managed products and index-based products, as demonstrated in Figure 41-1.

Few companies are purely good or evil

While you may not condone the particular activities of certain companies, the operations of these firms are not illegal. Meanwhile there are many "socially responsible" firms whose officers and employees have committed crimes in the supposed service of shareholders. Bribes, false claims, price-rigging, employee abuse, sexism, and other immoral, often illegal practices occur in many firms found within socially responsible portfolios. At the same time, how and where do we draw lines? Accepting the harm to health of smoking, should we consider the impact on health of sugared cereals, fatty foods and soda? Should oil companies and utilities with nuclear plants be derided while socially 'acceptable' firms who waste energy are praised?

Sharks take advantage of your good will

Wall Street firms who are smart enough to know the damage of inhibited investing nonetheless created socially responsible products to take advantage of your good will. Brokers profit from the sale of such products while they simultaneously assist the growth and finances of 'sinful' companies.

More broadly, the revenues and profits earned by any firm depend on the people who buy the products and services; not on those who own shares of stock. Socially guided investing has no effect on the behaviors considered irresponsible; it only steers outsized profits from those who care toward those who don't.

Figure 41-1: Socially Responsible Fund Performance 2001-2017

– – Vanguard 500 Index Fund   —— Vanguard FTSE Social Index Fund

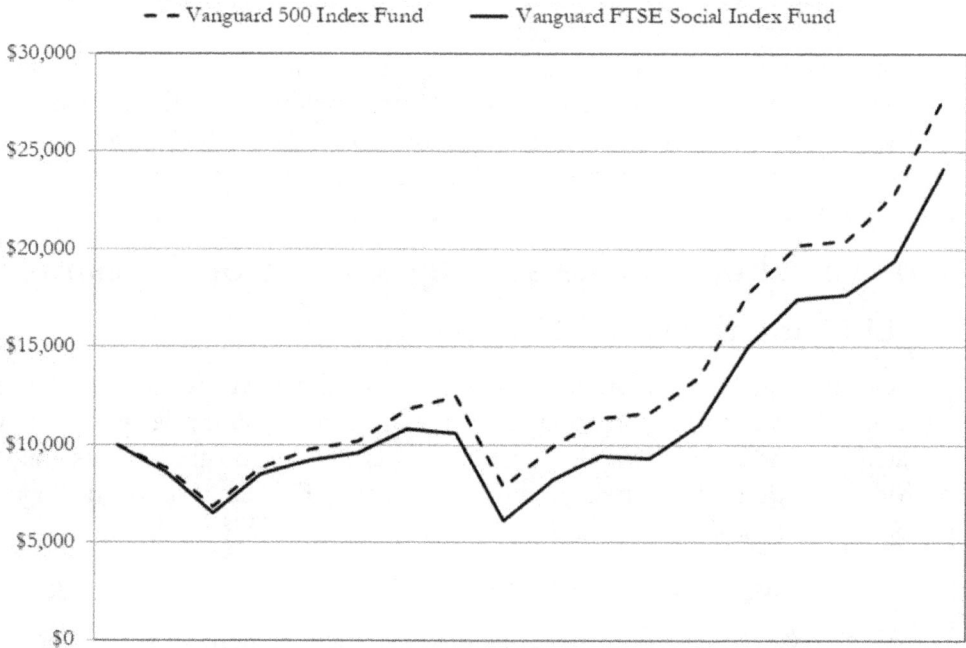

What you should do instead

First, stand up for your beliefs. If so inclined, guide loved ones toward healthy products. Support laws and lawmakers devoted to positive change, however you define it. Join boycotts and directly lobby firms to foster progress.

As for investing, your wellbeing is best served when you remain purely logical. If you hold socially responsible funds as part of a portfolio with which you are otherwise happy, you can immediately improve prospects by selling those holdings and replacing them with low expense, no-load index mutual funds or ETFs.

If socially responsible holdings represent your entire investment regimen, read Section IV for an ethical, logical, return maximizing route.

* Data source:
The Vanguard Group, Inc.

42: Timing Markets

What is market timing?

Market timing is the attempt to be fully invested when the market rises and not exposed when it falls. A more subdued strategy would avoid the all-or-nothing approach and revolve around a central asset allocation percentage; stocks would be over-weighted and under-weighted in anticipation of bull and bear markets, respectively. Basically, buy low and sell high. You do not have to find winners; you simply have to be invested at the right time.

Why you should avoid market timing

Most news leads us to bad timing

Anyone can look back in time, plot market levels and see 'lost' opportunities of buying in the valleys and selling near the peaks. Unfortunately, those valleys mark times when news is generally horrible and the world seems doomed to enter depression. Conversely, the peaks usually coincide with glowing news of profits, productivity and the promise of even better things to come. Unless you are completely oblivious to current events in general and business news in particular, you will be encouraged to buy and sell at the worst times.

There is no useful predictor of market turns

Every morning, analysts on business channels predict if the market will rise or fall during the trading day. These one-day prognosticators are wrong as often as they are right. The fact is: no one can know what the market will do next; this is true about tomorrow, next month, next year and beyond. Despite ads and brags to the contrary, no system predicting tops and bottoms actually works. If it did, computer programs would already be utilizing it and the owners wouldn't be telling you about it.

Missing only a few days of an upturn destroys results

Many people who try to time markets have invested at what looked like bottoms only to discover they bought near the top of a much bigger decline. More commonly, timers often hold back on buying stocks, waiting for a dip of some sort, only to miss out on most of the appreciation. Fact is, many of the market's best days come right after a trough when the world looks most bleak. Over the 50 years 1968 through 2017, there were over 12,000 trading days during which the S&P 500 had an average annual return of 10.05%.

Excluding only the best 50 days of that period, the average annual return for all 50 years drops more than half to 4.8%.

Figure 42-1: Annualized Stock Performance 1968 - 2017

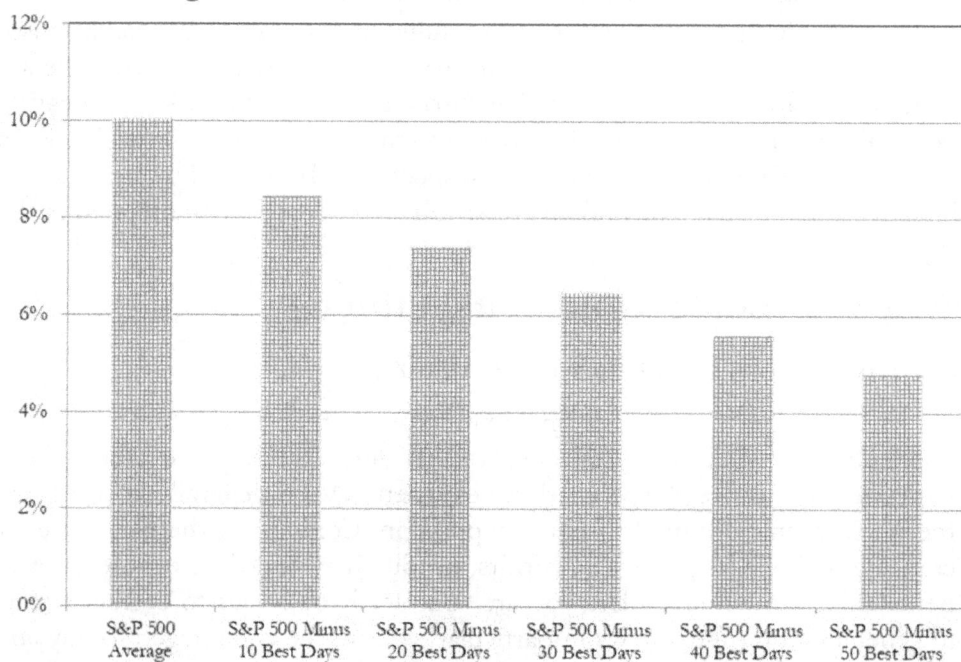

In dollar terms, the impact of lost opportunity is more dramatic. $10,000 invested in the S&P 500 at the beginning of 1968 and not touched for 50 years thereafter would have grown to about $1.2 million. If you missed only the best ten days of over 12,000 trading days, the ending balance would have been less than $600,000 instead. If you missed the best 50 days, you would have ended up with about $103,000.

Professional market timers do poorly

To succeed at market timing, guessing correctly more than half the time is not good enough. This is because you have stunted your returns during those times you are wrong, as cash is not as profitable as stocks in an up market. Research shows you must be right about 74% of the time to match the returns of a buy and hold strategy.

In a survey by CXO Advisory Group of Manassas, Virginia covering 68 professional timers from 2005 through 2012, only one firm hit the 70% success rate. Another study by the same group analyzing over 3,500 predictions by 34 firms from 2000 through 2012 found no firms did better than a 67% rate while 22 of the 34 were under 50%. Separately, Professors John Graham at the University of Utah and Campbell Harvey at Duke University looked at over 15,000 timing predictions by 237 newsletters from

1980 to 1992. The results of these newsletters were poor enough to drive 94% of them out of business during the period. These stats refer to professionals. What are your odds?

Figure 42-2: Growth of $10,000 in Stocks 1968 - 2017

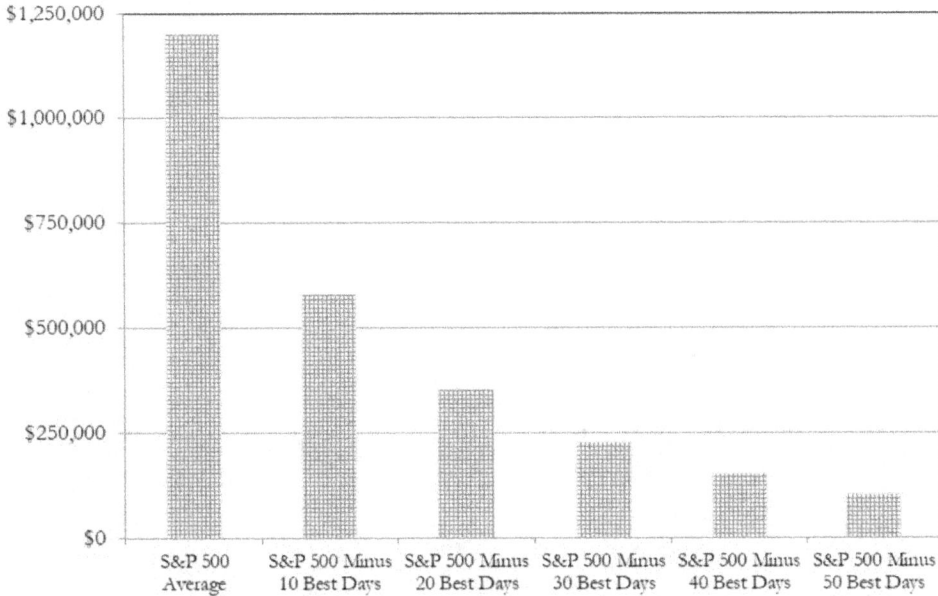

What you should do instead

Do not try to time the markets. If you have not already done so, evaluate your tolerance for risk (Chapter 45) and determine your appropriate target asset allocation (Chapter 46). Regardless of what you think about market tops and bottoms, you should bring your equity exposure toward your target allocation.

If you have no stock exposure at this point and are hesitant to jump in fully, pick a date within a year to achieve a fully invested position. Count the months between now and the date chosen. Divide the amount of money you will allocate to stocks by the number of months. Invest this dollar amount each month. If the market falls, you will buy at better prices. If it rises, what you already bought will have done well.

Know there will be ups and downs. You will save time and gain value not trying to predict when they occur.

* Data sources:
S&P Dow Jones Indices LLC; Standard & Poor's 500 Index, CXO Advisory Group, LLC
John Graham and Campbell Harvey, "Market Timing Ability and Volatility Implied in Investment Newsletters' Asset Allocation Recommendations," Journal of Financial Economics, vol. 42, no. 3 (1996)

Section IV

A Proper Investment Regimen

43: A Brief Guide

You don't need to know a lot to invest well. As long as you minimize expenses, properly allocate assets and avoid scams and imprudent practices you can grow your wealth better than most professional money managers.

Step 1: Define your goals

At minimum, you must meet life's necessary expenses, such as food, shelter and health. Most likely, you wish to achieve more than the minimum. You may want to live more comfortably, travel more, perhaps afford some major purchases, and/or provide a decent inheritance to your kids. Investing isn't gambling. It is a means to meet your goals most effectively. So know your goals.

Step 2: Assess your tolerance for risk

Investing should be a source of comfort and satisfaction, not angst and regret. Angst can come from declines in market value you did not count on. Regret can come from growing assets inadequately – the feeling you didn't take enough chances. Higher returns get you to your goals faster but seeking such entails greater risk. You need to be comfortable in your own investment skin. To get comfortable, you need to determine your personal risk profile: both your wealth and nerves will be well served.

Step 3: Determine an appropriate asset allocation

Knowing your risk tolerance, you can estimate an appropriate asset allocation: the target percentage mix of stocks and bonds. Your experiences over time may affect your comfort with volatility; you should adjust your target mix accordingly.

Step 4: Select an institution

When deciding where to hold your financial assets, be sure you can access your money and invest in securities best suited to meet your needs at minimum cost.

Step 5: Select securities

With your stock portfolio you can use index funds to track the market or rely on active management via funds or individual stocks. Similarly, with your bond portfolio you can choose index funds or active management of funds and/or individual bonds and CDs.

Optional: Select an advisor

You can easily do all five steps above. You can take a brief quiz to assess your risk profile, determine a fitting asset allocation from your profile, open an account at a good institution, buy no-load index funds (or other appropriate securities) to match your target allocation and, well-positioned, get on with the rest of your life.

Instead, you may want help with one or more of these steps. Advisor fees will reduce your returns, but you can choose to make that sacrifice to have someone else do the work. If so inclined, read Chapter 50. You want to be sure you are being served and not sold.

44: Define Your Financial Goals

The rest of this section deals with handling your money well. This one chapter addresses your goals; putting them in quantifiable terms and calculating how much you need to save to achieve them.

If your needs and wants are already well taken care of, you need only focus on maximizing returns and eliminating scams. You can skip this chapter.

If you have doubts about the ability of your financial resources to meet your needs and wants for the rest of your life, read on.

Understand your financial situation

You can easily discover the financial status of any publicly traded company by viewing its balance sheet and income statement. A balance sheet shows assets, debt and net worth as of a particular date. An income statement reports flows of income, expenses and the net change to your net worth during a particular period. In a very simple format, you should have similar cognizance of your own situation.

Figure 44-1: A Simple Personal Balance Sheet

Assets		Debt & Net Worth	
Cash	$1,000	Credit cards	5,000
Non-retirement accounts	$20,000	Car loans	15,000
IRA balances	$30,000	Student loans	30,000
Company 401k balances	$50,000	Mortgage	150,000
Total liquid assets	$101,000	Total debt	200,000
House	$300,000	**Net Worth**	**251,000**
Cars	$25,000	(equals total assets	
Other	$25,000	minus total debt)	
Total assets	$451,000	Total debt & net worth	451,000

To create your balance sheet, list the total balances from your bank, brokerage, and employer retirement statements. These are the "liquid" assets you can invest. Separately, list other substantial assets such as a home, car, collectibles and such. Estimate their value. The total of these estimates plus your liquid assets are your total assets. Now list all loan and credit card balances. Add these to get your total debt. Subtract total debt from total assets. The result is your net worth.

Going forward, income and asset growth will add to your worth. Investment losses and expenses – including financial fees and debt costs – will take away from it.

Figure 44-2: A Simple Personal Income Statement

Income	
Job related - wages, Social Security, pensions, disability, etc.	$75,000
Investment related - interest, dividends, capital gains, etc.	$10,000
Other - gifts, inheritance, gambling wins, etc.	$2,000
Total income	$87,000
Expenses	
Living - food, medical, clothing, transportation, taxes, etc.	$25,000
Home related - rent, mortgage interest, utilities, taxes, etc.	$20,000
Financial - sales fees, management fees, loan fees, interest, taxes, etc.	$15,000
Other - vacations, gifts, gambling losses, taxes, etc.	$10,000
Total expenses	$70,000
Net Income / change to net worth	$17,000

Know the key dollar figure you should aim for

As a minimum goal, you want your net worth to be a positive number when you pass after having paid for all of the things you need. A better goal: a positive net worth when you pass after having done all the things you want. Even better: do all those things and leave substantial net assets to others to help them achieve their goals and dreams.

Most of us face a life cycle with two adult financial phases: a period during which we earn money and add to our worth followed by retirement, a period in which we might find ourselves draining assets. There could be intermittent variations from that model, such as spans of unemployment or years in which big health or education expenses hit. But those financially rainy days are just bumpy parts of a road leading to the end of our working life. At some point, you will probably begin a long spell of reliance on non-wage income.

You may be able to keep wealth growing until your final days. If you are not yet in that position, if your anticipated expenses exceed your expected future income, before retirement your savings must get to a level adequate to meet your needs for the rest of your life.

What do you need?

To determine how much you need to invest, it is helpful to divide your financial goals between things you need versus those you want. Only you will know the difference.

For instance, you need money for food, shelter and medical expenses. You probably also need to cover the costs of transportation, insurance, education, maintenance, and clothing. Some minimal amount for recreation could also be considered a need.

Assign dollar amounts to these things. When in doubt as to "how much", choose higher amounts. While there will be good things not predicted in your budget, bad things happen, too.

What do you want?

Do you want to upgrade your 'needs', e.g. with a bigger home or more nights eating out? Do you want to travel more? Are there charitable causes you would like to advance? Do you want to enhance your children's wellbeing while you are around, and afterward?

For each dream there is a definable range of costs. Similar to planning for life's needs, you can add these costs into your calculations to help some dreams become reality.

How do you get there?

An online planning application or well-organized spreadsheet can help you calculate the amount you need to accumulate before retirement. Similar tools can assist the calculation of saving patterns needed to reach this amount and other goals, such as funding school or buying a home. You are encouraged to seek and utilize such tools.

But to provide a complete picture herewith, the rest of this chapter shows a framework you can use to estimate how much you will need upon retirement and how much you need to save before you get there. If you already have a grasp on your retirement resources or you are not in the mood for math, move on to Chapter 45. You can always come back.

How much will you need upon retirement?

When calculating what you need to save to cover retirement expenses, remember to factor in other resources such as Social Security and savings already accumulated.

Figure 44-3: Needed Accumulation for $1,000 in Monthly Expenses

Retirement	ROR					
Age	0%	1%	3%	5%	7%	9%
60	480,000	395,482	279,342	207,384	160,919	129,641
65	420,000	354,251	259,841	198,142	156,530	127,552
70	360,000	310,907	237,189	186,282	150,308	124,282
75	300,000	265,342	210,876	171,060	141,487	119,162
80	240,000	217,441	180,311	151,525	128,983	111,145

Moving forward, Figure 44-3 shows how much you need to accumulate by retirement to cover $1,000 per month in expenses until you are 100 years old. You can see the impact of retiring at different ages and the effect of earning different rates of return.

For example, if you stop working at age 70 and earn 5% going forward, a balance of $186,282 as of your retirement date would provide income of $1,000 per month for the next 30 years. If you stopped work at 65 and earn only 3% in the years ensuing, you'd need $259,841 in the account to pull out $1,000 per month for the next 35 years.

How much more do you need to accumulate?

You may already have assets invested. In the same way Social Security helps cover expenses, your accumulated savings bring you closer to targeted future goals. Figure 44-4 shows how $10,000 currently invested grows over time with various return assumptions.

Figure 44-4: Growth of $10,000

Years	ROR					
	0%	1%	3%	5%	7%	9%
5	10,000	10,510	11,593	12,763	14,026	15,386
10	10,000	11,046	13,439	16,289	19,672	23,674
20	10,000	12,202	18,061	26,533	38,697	56,044
30	10,000	13,478	24,273	43,219	76,123	132,677
40	10,000	14,889	32,620	70,400	149,745	314,094

With 30 years left to retirement, Figure 44-4 shows that at 5% your $10,000 will grow to $43,219. At 7%, your $10,000 would instead grow to $76,123.

How much should you save to reach your target?

Figure 44-5 shows the amount you need to save each month to accumulate $100,000 at some point in the future. You can see the impact of time and different rates of return.

Figure 44-5: Monthly Deposits Needed to Accumulate $100,000

Years	ROR					
	0%	1%	3%	5%	7%	9%
5	1,667	1,626	1,547	1,470	1,397	1,326
10	833	793	716	644	578	517
20	417	377	305	243	192	150
30	278	238	172	120	82	55
40	208	170	108	66	38	21

If you're 40 now and plan to retire at 70 you have 30 years to save. If your investments earn 7%, saving $82 per month would get your portfolio from nothing to $100,000. If you earn only 3% instead, you would need to put away $172 per month to get to $100,000 over the same period.

Example 1: Putting this all together

Assume you are 40 years old, plan to retire at 70, have $50,000 saved for retirement and expect Social Security benefits of $2,000 per month. You estimate desired retirement spending to be about $5,000 per month. Analyzing your tolerance for risk (Chapter 45), you see the proportion of stocks and bonds appropriate for you historically averaged 5% returns (Appendix C). Under these assumptions, what do you need to start saving each month to make retirement everything you want it to be?

Your desired retirement lifestyle of $5,000 per month is partly offset by Social Security of $2,000; you will need your financial assets to generate $3,000 per month from the time you are 70 until you are 100. Using Figure 44-3, 5% returns and the 70 retirement age, you see $186,282 is needed for $1,000 per month. For $3,000, you'll need to accumulate three times $186,282, or $558,846.

You already have $50,000 in your portfolio. Figure 44-4 shows $10,000 growing to $43,219 in 30 years at 5%. Your $50,000 would grow to five times that number, or $216,095. Thus means $216,095 of your $558,846 target is already taken care of. Your new savings need only grow to the difference, $342,751.

Lastly, referring to Figure 44-5, $120 deposited monthly earning 5% will grow to $100,000 in 30 years. Since you need to raise $342,751 by then, multiply $120 by 3.42751 ($342,751 divided by $100,000) to get $411– the amount you should put away each month.

Summarizing this example, depositing $411 each month into investments earning 5% for the next 30 years produces an ending balance of $342,751. Your current balance of $50,000 already invested at 5% will grow to $216,095. Those two balances add up to $558,846. This $558,846 will allow withdrawals of $3,000 per month from age 70 through age 100, supplementing Social Security payments of $2,000 for total monthly income of $5,000. So under these assumptions, saving $411 each month starting now will allow your retirement to be all that you want it to be.

Round numbers to save time and gain security

No one knows what the future holds. The rate of return on your portfolio will not be exactly 5% or any other guessed number. The economy will flourish and falter. Your budget will change, as will tax laws and life expectancy. Meanwhile health, opportunity and technology may affect your retirement date.

The calculations described so far may be accurate, but they represent guideposts to mark minimums. To ease the math and build a cushion, round up your expenses and round down your returns.

Example 2: A simplified approach

Consider the example just cited: You are 40 years old, have $50,000 saved, expect 5% returns, and hope to retire at 70 with Social Security benefits of $2,000 per month and anticipated retirement expenses of $5,000 per month.

Figure 44-6: Examples of Calculating Goal-Achieving Savings

Line	Description	Calculation	"Accurate" Information	Rounded Information
1	Desired retirement expenses	Your input	$5,000	$5,000
2	Non-Investment income	Your input	$2,000	$2,000
3	Expenses not covered	Line 1 - Line 2	$3,000	$3,000
4	Balance needed per $1,000 (Age 70, 5%)	From Table 50-1	$186,282	$200,000
5	Uncovered expenses divided by $1,000	Line 3 / 1,000	3	3
6	Balance you need at retirement	Line 4 x Line 5	$558,846	$600,000
7	Current savings	Your input	$50,000	$50,000
8	Future value of $10,000 (30 years, 5%)	From Table 50-2	$43,219	$40,000
9	Your savings divided by $10,000	Line 7 / 10000	5	5
10	Future value of your savings	Line 8 x Line9	$216,095	$200,000
11	Net balance needed from new savings	Line 6 - Line 10	$342,751	$400,000
12	Monthly deposits per $100,000 (30 Years, 5%)	From Table 50-3	$120	$120
13	Net Balance Needed divided by $100,000	Line 11 / 100,000	3.42751	4
14	New Monthly Deposits Needed	Line 12 x Line 13	$411	$480

Per $1,000 in monthly income, Figure 44-3 indicates a needed retirement balance of $186,282 (age 70, 5% ROR). Round this up to $200,000, and then multiply by 3 for the $3,000 excess expense you seek to cover. This gives you a target accumulation of $600,000.

Addressing your current savings, Figure 44-4 indicates $10,000 grows to $43,219 after 30 years at 5%. Round this down to $40,000, then multiply by five (you have five times $10,000) to estimate an ending value of $200,000. Subtracting this from your needed accumulation of $600,000, your target future balance for new savings is $400,000.

Looking at Figure 44-5, you find $120 per month will grow to $100,000 at 5% over 30 years. You need $400,000, so you should start saving $480 ($120 times 4) per month to meet your goals, with much room for error. Of course, you are always encouraged to save more than the formulas indicate, with or without rounding.

Now, knowing how much to save, the rest of this section will help you invest it well.

45: Assess Your Risk Tolerance

In the long run stocks outperform bonds and cash. So why not put your entire portfolio into equities? For one, who wants to put all their money into something that can and did drop more than 30% in the course of a year? Remember the crash of 1987, or the internet bust in 2000 or the financial meltdown in 2008? How about the "lost decade", the first ten years of the current millennium during which large-cap stocks provided no return?

Consider the other end of the spectrum. There are investments in which no one ever lost money, such as FDIC insured bank accounts and U.S. treasury bonds held until maturity. Very safe, but there have been spells during which they failed to keep up with inflation. We save and invest to grow wealth. Who wants to park money in a vehicle practically assured of losing spending power?

To limit potential damage from any single pitfall, you are best served by a mix of stocks and bonds versus an all-or-nothing approach. How much to put into each asset class is the essence and end result of an assessment of your risk tolerance.

You may already know your risk profile. Perhaps you completed a questionnaire online or with a broker. Maybe after decades of investing you know the proportions of stocks and bonds you like to hold. If so, feel free to move on to Chapter 47.

A brief quiz

If you are unclear about your tolerance for investment related risk, consider the following three questions:

Question One: Which of the following statements best describes your view?

1) I do not want to have losses. I do not mind accepting rates of return below the rate of inflation as long as the value of my accounts never decline.
2) I do not like volatility and I certainly do not want to see my account fall over the course of a year, though I would like a chance to earn more than bank CD rates.
3) I want to beat inflation and build up the real value of my account. I hope interest and dividends earned make up for any annual downside risk.
4) I would like a good balance of income and growth. I seek decent appreciation and can accept a slight loss of value in any given quarter or year.
5) I know stocks are the best vehicle for growing wealth. I want to take advantage, but I want to keep some powder dry and have a bond component to reduce potential downward fluctuations.

6) I want my assets to have a chance to earn the highest returns possible. I will probably experience great volatility and spells of huge loss. But in the long run, I trust a 100% stock allocation will serve me best.

Question Two: What is the largest single year loss you would be willing to absorb in an investment without losing faith in that vehicle's viability and appropriateness for your portfolio?

1) None - I do not want anything that can go down, ever.
2) I could stand a loss of 5% over the course of a year, but not much more.
3) I could take a temporary 10% hit, but I would watch carefully after that.
4) A drop of 15% would sting, but I am in it for the long run.
5) I could lose 20% and not blink. Above that, I may pay more attention.
6) Any temporary loss is fine. Often the greater the risk, the greater the ultimate return.

Question Three: Figure 45-1 displays the average, best and worst annualized returns over the past 50 years of six investment choices. Review how they performed over time. If you had to commit all of your retirement assets to one of these six choices for a full decade, which investment would you select?

Figure 45-1: Historical Returns of Asset Mixes 1968-2017

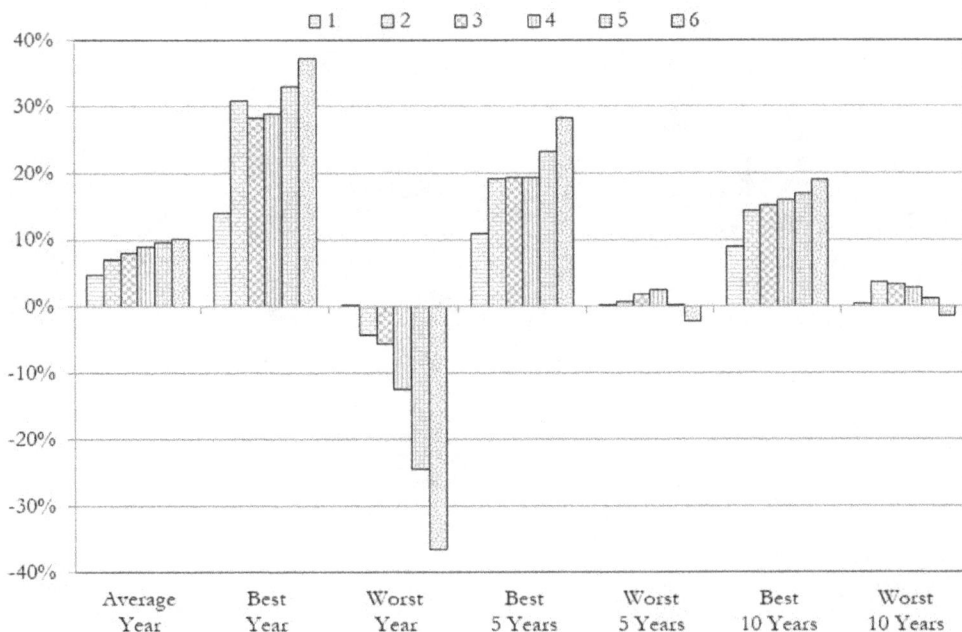

Quizzes like this help you determine and quantify your tolerance for risk. For instance, answering '1' to any of the questions above indicates great aversion to risk; answering '6' shows extreme tolerance. Such quantification can lead directly to a logical asset allocation.

46: Allocate Assets

Over time, the allocation of assets between stocks, bonds and cash will be the major determinant of the rate of return of your portfolio. If you hold bonds only, even great bonds, you will probably not achieve growth obtainable with stocks. If you hold stocks only, even shares of very stable firms like utilities and established food brands, your portfolio will be subject to occasionally dramatic declines. You will be well-served owning a mix of stocks and bonds. The mix should not be random but based on your tolerance for risk. Since stocks generally provide better returns in the long run, you want to maximize your stock holdings, but only insofar as you are comfortable with the extra volatility.

You may already know what percentage you want to invest in stocks and bonds. If this percentage is based on prior analysis or extensive experience owning securities, you are probably correct. Feel free to skip the rest of this chapter.

If you have not recently analyzed your risk profile, if you have yet to experience an entire investment cycle with bull and bear markets, or if your portfolio lacks either stocks or bonds, assess your tolerance.

Chapter 45 includes a short quiz. Perhaps too brief to judge an entire regimen, it is nonetheless demonstrative and calibrated to convert risk-related views to a reasonable asset allocation.

If you have not done so already, answer the three questions posed. Add the values of your three answers. For example, if you answered "3) I want to beat inflation…", "4) A temporary drop of 15%", and "4) Investment 4", your total would be 11 (3+4+4). Multiply this number by 5% to arrive at a suggested target stock allocation. As 11 times 5% equals 55%, a target stock allocation of about 55% is indicated. This should not be regarded as a recommendation or even a precise figure to aim for. It is just one input to help you understand the process and determine an appropriate range.

There are online tools which can help you gauge an appropriate asset allocation. You may also find it helpful to peruse the chart in Appendix C which displays historical return data for asset allocations from 0% stocks through 100% stocks, with the rest in bonds.

If over time you find your portfolio too volatile or not gainful enough, consider adjusting your asset allocation appropriately. Experience should supersede a test and a chart.

47: Select Institution(s)

Many people choose investments based on what's available at the institution where their money sits. The process should be the opposite. You want to figure out what investments you plan to hold and then pick the best institution where you can hold them.

Securities available

For stocks and bonds, you are best served by a discount brokerage. You will have access to all the securities and services of a full-service broker but at far less cost.

If you seek index ETFs, many discount brokers such as E-Trade and TD Ameritrade provide access to very low expense exchange traded funds free of trading costs. Some firms such as Fidelity, Schwab and Vanguard also offer excellent low-cost proprietary index ETFs.

If you seek mutual funds, the best discount brokers have excellent platforms with a wide choice of no-load index and managed funds. You can also buy low cost, no-load mutual funds directly through fund families.

For CDs, many discount brokerages have platforms wherein you can find the highest rates in the country. If your needs are simple, local banks provide convenient, if sub-maximal, choices.

Needed services

For paying bills and getting cash, you will need a bank or an institution with banking services. Some discount brokers like Schwab provide all these services at low or no cost. Most financial institutions now allow you to link your accounts, internally and at other firms. Thanks to these links, you should be able to invest anywhere and bank anywhere with unhindered convenience. You need not invest with a sales-fee laden outfit simply because its reps have desks at your bank.

Cost

With assured access to the securities and services you need, minimizing expense is vital. The worst practitioners on Wall Street rip off their clients by passing off their high fees and commissions as normal costs of doing business. Deregulation, competition and technology have enabled well run companies to reduce trading costs dramatically and provide many services free of charge. With identical market and exchange related costs, the only reason one firm charges more than another for financial services is abject greed.

Don't be victimized. Choose an institution that charges nothing to open and maintain an account, nothing to buy and sell mutual funds, and less than $10 to execute stock trades. Refer to Appendix A for suggestions.

48: Select Stock Investments

To achieve your targeted allocation to stocks, you can invest in mutual funds, exchange traded funds and individual equities. Logic and research both highlight the efficacy of low cost index funds. You could put your entire equity allocation into a low-cost no-load index equity mutual fund or ETF and be done – and done well – with your stock decision making.

But other factors may lead you to do otherwise. Best practices specific to each vehicle are presented separately. The comments on diversification and capitalization apply to all.

Diversify overall

Never invest more than 5% of your portfolio in any single firm. If you hold mutual funds or ETFs exclusively, you are naturally diversified. You could put 95% of your assets in a fund and 5% into a specific stock and still be considered well diversified. If you only own individual stocks, you should have at least 20 of them. More would be better. You do not want your wealth significantly damaged through the poor performance of any single firm.

Diversify in detail

Even if you own funds or more than 20 stocks, you still could be susceptible to the unique risk of a sector or region. Familiarity or preference for a particular attribute such as dividend yield could lead you to concentrate assets imprudently.

Regarding industry exposure, Standard and Poor's divides companies into ten major groupings: consumer discretionary, consumer staples, energy, finance, health care, industrial, information technology, materials, telecommunications and utilities. Broad index funds will own all of these. If you invest in sector funds or individual stocks, spread out. If you invest abroad, you might want to keep exposure to any individual country below 20%.

Consider large-cap firms your core

A firm's capitalization is its market value, which is equal to the price of its stock times the number of shares outstanding. To guide investor expectations, companies are divided into capitalization categories. Though additional distinctions such as "mega" and "micro" get used, for the most part we invest in a universe of large-, mid- and small-cap firms.

The dividing lines can be blurry, and they go up over time as market values rise. As of this edition, a reasonable grouping would define large-cap firms as those with a market value above $10 billion, small-cap as firms valued under $2 billion, and mid-cap firms in between.

Large-cap corporations are huge. Most have been around for quite some time. Since you invest for the long haul, it can be of great comfort to know a firm has been and probably will be around for decades.

Small- and mid-cap stocks present potentially higher returns but greater volatility. Many of these firms fail, though others grow dramatically. Given their increased uncertainty, keep your exposure to each of these lower than your exposure to large-cap firms.

Stock mutual funds

Consider index funds first – perhaps only

Possibly the most efficient and profitable means to populate your stock allocation is utilizing index funds. Indexes have outpaced 90% of managed mutual funds in spans of 20 years or more.

The simplest investment is to put all of your equity money in just a few, maybe just one, broad index fund. Instead, you can get more involved with indexed exposure to specific sectors or countries. If you are tempted to invest in a fund not of the low-cost no-load index variety, avoid the pitfalls highlighted in Chapters 18 through 31.

Minimize expenses

Research has identified the expense ratio as the single most influential factor determining relative performance between similarly invested mutual funds. One study conducted by a mutual fund rating firm found expenses to be even more predictive than the firm's own rating system. Whether you use index or managed funds, going with the least costly choices in any investment category should serve you well.

Related, rule out all funds and fund platforms that charge or entail sales commissions.

Take size into account

For index funds, bigger is better. It is easier for a fund to match the contents of an index and smoothly handle shareholder transactions with a larger asset pool.

For managed money, bigger is not better. As you seek the benefits – real or perceived – of a specific stock picking team, you want their decisions to be effective. When a fund grows, the inclusion of an increasing number of securities causes its properties to progressively simulate an index, minus expenses.

Stock exchange traded funds

Consider index ETFs only

As discussed in Chapter 29, managed mutual funds historically provide inferior returns versus index funds. This underperformance occurs despite perfect knowledge of each day's net cash flow; mutual fund shares transact only after the market closes. ETF shares transact during market hours. Net cash flows are unknown until each instant investors buy and sell the ETF shares. With unknown cash flow and trading needs, a managed ETF is not likely to do as well as a managed mutual fund. Since the latter do not do well period, in the world of ETFs you are especially wise to stick with index choices.

Minimize expenses

Index ETFs are each intended to track the performance of a specific index. To the extent ETFs incur costs there will be some drag on performance. If two ETFs track the same index and have very different expense ratios, select the one with least expense.

Don't overpay for the assets

While mutual fund shares transact at the precise net asset value (NAV) of the underlying securities, ETF shares transact at prices determined through the bid/ask process of the stock market. You do not want to overpay for anything.

So, when considering an ETF, navigate to the issuer's site, look up the net asset value per share of the ETF under consideration and compare that NAV to the current market price. If the NAV is at or above the purchase price, you should feel comfortable moving forward. If the NAV is more than a few percentage points less than the price, find a more fairly priced ETF with the same exposure. If none exist, seek a mutual fund tracking the same index.

When all else is the same, favor larger funds

If you need to decide between two ETFs with the same target index, similar expense ratios and dramatically different sizes, choose the larger one. First, a larger asset pool makes it easier to emulate the contents of an index. Second, the price of an ETF is established in the open market through the same 'bid and ask' process of stocks. Small ETFs are more apt to trade at higher spreads, rendering lower prices when selling or higher prices when buying.

Individual stocks

If you have enough money, and the gumption, to buy 20 or more stock positions, you can build your own portfolio. This is not recommended; research, liquidity, risk and other factors favor index funds. Still, you may want to pick some of your own stocks. Whatever the reasons, the admonitions below are precautions intended to limit your downside risk and not advice to seek or buy any particular equity.

Don't try to win the lottery

It is hard to find big winners. Many revolutionary products are brought out by private firms. If something of material importance is on the horizon for a public company, insiders and analysts researching the firm will discover it long before you. By the time you can buy into something new and exciting, the price probably already reached a level at which insiders would rather sell. If a broker is presenting an idea to you, you can be sure there's a reason his firm is not simply keeping it for themselves.

Don't ignore the numbers

When you buy a stock, you are buying future earnings. You are not buying cars, movies, airplanes, banks or really cool websites. Through ownership of a security, you have rights to a portion of future earnings, however and wherever those earnings are generated. If you pay a lot for a given level of expected earnings, you will probably not fare as well as you would have if you paid less for the same expected level. A low PE (price to earnings) ratio is good. A low PEG (price to earnings to growth) ratio is better. There are a host of metrics you can consider and helpful websites you can visit. If you are picking stocks in lieu of index funds, you should know why. Keep the numbers in your favor.

Ignore ads and cold calls

If someone you never met had an extremely profitable method to pick stocks, he or she would not tell you about it. Even if such a system did exist, it couldn't last. Given the natural effects of supply and demand, if a large group of people used the same system, as they buy and sell the same securities prices would rapidly adjust to wipe out the system's benefits. Never buy any security based on a tip or sales pitch, especially if it comes from someone you do not know.

49: Select Bond Investments

Similar to stocks, you can build your bond portfolio with mutual funds, exchange traded funds and individual bonds. Unlike stocks, there are advantages to owning individual bonds and CDs instead of funds (Chapter 21). The following passages will help you achieve excellent income with safety, regardless of the type of security you use.

Individual bonds

Keep maturities short

Under normal circumstances, yields on bonds get higher when their maturity extends farther into the future. Nonetheless, resist the temptation to garner yield with very long maturities.

First, long-term bonds are very volatile. When rates rise, long-term bonds will drop in value by substantially more than short-term bonds. If you ever had to sell before maturity, the losses could wipe out all previous income.

Second, you may have locked in a lousy rate for a very long time. Even if you think rates might go down, bonds are not for speculative investment. You are more secure and agile in terms of accessing new rates if you buy short and intermediate term bonds. Limit purchases to maturities of seven years or less.

Keep maturities spread out

To reduce risk and maintain flexibility, build your portfolio with bonds of different maturities. You may see the term "ladder" used to describe such a pattern. Some brokerage bond platforms have tools to help you build bond ladders.

For example, as you create a portfolio from scratch you might buy bonds maturing in one, two, three, four, and five years. In a year, the 1-year bond will mature, the 2-year bond will age and become a 1-year bond, the 3-year bond will become a 2-year bond, and so on. If you take the proceeds from the maturation of the former 1-year bond and buy a new 5-year bond, your laddered portfolio will be back to its original one to five-year structure.

You do not have to achieve perfect form. If you can earn more buying a bond maturing in 30 months instead of a similar one maturing in 24 or 36 months, buy the 30-month bond. However, do not put your entire portfolio into the longest maturity of your range simply because the rates at that end are highest. Spread out but be flexible.

Seek investment grade bonds

The bond portion of your portfolio is intended to provide income and reduce overall volatility. You want to buy securities you will not have to worry about. Avoid non-investment grade (a.k.a. 'junk' or 'high yield') bonds. Instead, seek securities classified as "investment grade" by the major credit agencies. All bonds issued by the U.S. government (a.k.a. treasuries) and government sponsored enterprises (a.k.a. agencies) are so rated. Along with FDIC insured CDs, you should feel very secure investing in treasuries and agencies.

Many corporate bonds are also rated investment grade. Corporates usually offer higher yields than government related bonds, so a little extra work may be worthwhile.

Diversify when not insured by the government

You could put all of your money into a single treasury bond or up to $250,000 into an FDIC insured bank CD without issuer risk concern. Among corporates, even if you limit your holdings to the most secure names, don't put all your eggs into one basket. Limit exposure in any one company to 5% of your bond portfolio.

Bond mutual funds

Per comments in Chapter 21, bond mutual funds may not be as effective as individual bonds and CDs. But you may nonetheless need to invest in funds. They may be the only choice in a retirement plan or education savings platform; the asset level in an account may be insufficient for a diversified portfolio; you may prefer simplicity to effectiveness. Whatever your reason, the following comments should help.

Minimize expenses

Expense ratios are the biggest determinant of relative performance between similarly invested mutual funds. This is particularly true of bond funds, where costs can take a big bite out of interest income. When choosing between bond funds of the same maturity range and credit quality, if there's no compelling reason to do otherwise pick the one with least expense. Related, rule out all funds and fund platforms that charge sales commissions.

Seek bonds you would buy individually

Your bond portfolio should be a source of income and safety. To control risk, limit your fund choices to investment grade bonds with an average maturity less than seven years.

Bond exchange traded funds

Similar to mutual funds, ETFs may not be as effective as direct ownership of individual bonds and CDs, at least in terms of income and stability (Chapter 21). Still, you may prefer ETFs or be forced to select such in a platform. The suggestions below should be of benefit.

Minimize expenses

ETFs track the performance of a specific index, minus expenses. If two ETFs track the same index and have very different expense ratios, select the one with least expense.

Seek bonds you would buy individually

As stated previously, your allocation to fixed income should be a source of income and safety. Limit your ETF choices to investment grade bonds with short maturities.

Seek value by paying less for assets

Mutual fund shares transact at the precise net asset value (NAV) of the underlying securities. ETFs transact at a price determined by the market through offers and bids; the same as stocks.

When you narrow down your list of potential bond ETFs, for each navigate to the issuer's site and look up the net asset value per share. Compare each NAV to the current market price. If the NAV is at or above the purchase price, you should feel comfortable moving forward. If the NAV is less than the price, do not purchase. If no ETFs of the type you seek are available at a fair price, buy a mutual fund in the same category instead.

50: If Needed, Select an Advisor

Unfortunately, anyone who can squeeze out a score of 70% on a relatively easy multiple-choice exam can be a financial advisor. Many practicing advisors have no formal education in finance or portfolio management. You should avoid these "professionals" in the same way you would avoid a "doctor" who never studied medicine.

You should also be cautious investing through individuals for whom investing is a secondary vocation. Such include bankers, insurance agents, planners and even some lawyers and accountants. Many of these individuals sell products with sales fees.

Below are some pointers to help you discern what type of help you need, and where best to get it.

Do you need an advisor for stocks?

Research and logic point to the ineffectiveness of active equity portfolio management (Chapter 29). If you agree, the money you allocate to stocks should be invested in index funds. You do not need an advisor to accomplish this. You may want assistance completing forms and executing your purchases; the good discount brokers and no-load fund families have staff on hand who will help you free of charge.

If you believe active management can improve your situation, perhaps for reasons of tax efficiency, capital preservation, or other goals well-served by hands-on attention, then hiring a registered investment advisor could make sense.

Do you need an advisor for bonds?

If you invest in bond funds, you do not need an advisor. As with stock index funds, any questions you might have about paperwork or finding a low-cost investment grade fund can be fielded by counselors at a discount broker or no-load fund family.

There are advantages to investing in individual bonds and CDs instead of funds (Chapter 21). You can easily build a quality portfolio. But if you do not want the fuss of screening for credit and maturity, and you do not mind the sacrifice of income that will be absorbed by fees, you might prefer the services of an RIA.

What to look for in an advisor

Only consider fiduciaries

Ask RIAs you contact if they are legally, officially, fiduciaries. If not, move on.

A fiduciary must act in your interest. Efforts must be made to ascertain your risk profile. The portfolio built must meet standards of suitability. If anything goes wrong with regard to conduct, inappropriate holdings or excessive fees, as long as the advisor professes fiduciary status you will have recourse.

Only work with portfolio managers

It is not prudent to pay twice for the same service. If you pay fees to an RIA to manage your money, you should not also pay mutual fund management companies or outside consultants to manage your money.

To judge whether or not an RIA is a portfolio manager, request a sample of holdings. If you see managed mutual funds, or hedge funds, or groupings of stocks with category names indicating outside management, drop this RIA from consideration.

The best RIAs invest in individual stocks and bonds. Some decent RIAs use index exchange traded funds and no-load index mutual funds.

Seek pertinent qualifications

To assess the intellectual qualifications of an RIA, ignore easily obtained credentials like the C.F.P. (Certified Financial Planner) or C.R.P.C. (Chartered Retirement Planning Counselor). The ability to temporarily recall seven of ten terms on a one-time test is not a skillset on which you should trust your assets. Your RIA should have studied finance at a high level. An M.B.A. (Master of Business Administration) with a concentration in finance is preferable. C.F.A. (Chartered Financial Analyst) certification is also a worthy designation.

Minimize fees

Drop from consideration any RIA who executes trades through a high cost institution. Fees for simply having an account, trading costs above $19, and the presence of B-share and C-share mutual funds are all signs of institutions, and RIAs, you should avoid. Only work with RIAs who situate your money at established, SIPC insured discount brokerages such as Schwab, TD Ameritrade and Vanguard.

Regarding fees to the RIA, similar to actively managed mutual funds, irrelevant past performance is often presented as an excuse to overcharge. The fee charged by RIAs who build portfolios of stocks and bonds need not be higher than 1% of assets. The fee charged by RIAs who use exchange traded funds and no-load index mutual funds should be far less, 0.5% of assets at most. If all other attributes are about the same, minimizing fees will work strongly to your benefit.

Compare

Most RIAs are excellent at describing what they do. It is easy to be convinced you have found the right firm at your first meeting. Investigate several RIAs before deciding.

Demand experience

In the markets, there is no substitute for experience. Be certain the RIA you hire to watch over your wealth has successfully managed portfolios through bull and bear markets, economic growth and recession, calm times and crises. Ask for detailed performance histories. Even if all other attributes line up nicely, in the end results are what matter. Remember, you can always opt for index funds.

Consider robots

If you agree index funds and cost minimization are best, but you want help determining an appropriate asset allocation and seek confidence your money is properly put to work, a robo-advisor might be a good option. On a robo-advisor's website, you provide information in the same manner you would sitting with a human advisor. The robo software takes your information, determines a risk appropriate portfolio, and invests your money in that portfolio.

Robo-advisors are not necessarily free or completely benign. They usually charge a fee. Some do not utilize low cost index funds. A few robo-advisors are merely mechanisms to bring assets into a particular firm where salespeople can then push commissionable products.

Thus, if you decide robo-advisors are right for you, shop around. Make sure your chosen platform uses only low-cost index funds, whether ETFs or no-load mutual funds. Minimize your fees; you can easily find platforms in which the combined fund and robo-advisor fees total less than 0.5%.

Some discount brokers such as Schwab have added robo-advisors to their lineup. Betterment and Wealthfront are independent robo-advisors also worthy of consideration.

51: Summary – Trust Yourself, not Wall Street

Your investments are there to help you and your family. Much of the Wall Street community sees things differently. They see your assets as resources to be tapped for their own benefit.

Most investment products reduce your expected returns through excessive fees and sales commissions. Many products add unwarranted risk and imprudence. Certain securities are flat out gambles and not investments at all.

Your financial plan of action should be to prevent harm and only do things beneficial to your health and wealth. Both will be served if you avoid all scams, minimize costs, and spend as little time as possible dealing with matters of money.

If you own anything in Section II, sell it. If you do anything in Section III, stop it. Ignore all investment related advertisements, phone calls, tips, and free dinner invitations. Either on your own or with the help of a fee-only fiduciary RIA, move your money to a low-cost institution; invest per the principals outlined in Section IV, and – with a wealth-maximizing risk appropriate portfolio working on your behalf – get on with the rest of your life.

Section V

Appendices

Appendix A: Excellent Low-Cost Institutions

The list of institutions in Figure A-1 is provided to set a bar. No institution is specifically recommended. However, the policies these institutions present are consistent with the purpose of growing your wealth. Key features include no account maintenance fees, free access to low-cost no-load mutual funds, and trade commission rates under $10.

There are other fine institutions. Compare their features and costs to those here, and act logically. See Chapter 47 for more comments.

Figure A-1: Excellent Low Cost Institutions

Firm	Very Low Cost Index Mutual Funds	Commission Free ETFs	Local Branches	Free Bank Services
E*TRADE		Y		Y
Fidelity	Y	Y	Y	Y
Schwab	Y	Y	Y	Y
TD Ameritrade		Y	Y	Y
Vanguard	Y	Y		

Appendix B: Low Cost Index Funds

As with the institutions shown in Appendix A, the list of funds below is provided to set a bar. No specific security is recommended.

However, if you construct a portfolio using the securities listed below at the firms listed – or others with the same expense and investment structure – you can be confident you are minimizing costs and maximizing expected returns in the asset categories chosen.

Figure B-1: Index Mutual Funds in Broad Categories

Security Group	Very Low Cost No Transaction Fees			No Transaction Fees	
	Fidelity	Schwab	Vanguard	E*TRADE	TD
Bond	FBIDX	SWLBX	VFICX	DBIRX	DBIRX
Large-Cap	FUSEX	SWPPX	VLACX	NOSIX	SVSPX
Mid-Cap	FSCLX	PESPX	VIMSX	NOMIX	NTIAX
Small-Cap	FSSPX	SWSSX	NAESX	NSIDX	DISSX
International	FSIIX	SWISX	VGTSX	NOINX	TRIEX

Figure B-2: Index ETFs in Broad Categories

Security Group	Vanguard	Schwab	Fidelity	TD Ameritrade
Bond	BND	SCHZ	AGG	BND
Large-Cap	VV	SCHX	IVV	IVV
Mid-Cap	VO	SCHM	IJH	VO
Small-Cap	VB	SCHA	IJR	VB
International	VEU	SCHF	IXUS	VEU

Figure B-3: Index Mutual Funds in Detailed Size/Style Categories

Security Group	Very Low Cost No Transaction Fees			No Transaction Fees	
	Fidelity	Schwab	Vanguard	E*TRADE	TD
Short Bonds		SWBDX	VFSTX		
Int. Bonds	FBIDX	SWLBX	VFICX	DBIRX	DBIRX
Long Bonds			VWESX		
Large Core	FUSEX	SWPPX	VLACX	NOSIX	SVSPX
Large Growth	FNCMX		VIGRX		TRCVX
Large Value		SFLNX	VIVAX	SFLNX	TRIRX
Mid Core	FSCLX	PESPX	VIMSX	NOMIX	NTIAX
Mid Growth			VMGRX		
Mid Value			VMVIX		
Small Core	FSSPX	SWSSX	NAESX	NSIDX	DISSX
Small Growth			VISGX		
Small Value			VISVX		
International	FSIIX	SWISX	VGTSX	NOINX	TRIEX

Figure B-4: Index ETFs in Detailed Size/Style Categories

Security Group	Vanguard	Schwab	Fidelity	TD Ameritrade
Short Bonds	BSV	SCHO	ISTB	BSV
Intermediate Bonds	BIV	SCHZ	AGG	BIV
Long Bonds	BLV	TLO	ILTB	BLV
Large Cap Core	VV	SCHX	IVV	IVV
Large Cap Growth	VUG	SCHG	IWF	VUG
Large Cap Value	VTV	SCHV	IVE	VTV
Mid Cap Core	VO	SCHM	IJH	VO
Mid Cap Growth	VOT	MDYG	IJK	VOT
Mid Cap Value	VOE	MDYV	IJJ	VOE
Small Cap Core	VB	SCHA	IJR	VB
Small Cap Growth	VBK	SLYG	IJT	VBK
Small Cap Value	VBR	SLYV	IJS	VBR
International	VEU	SCHF	IXUS	VEA

Figure B-5: Very Low Cost Transacton Fee Free Index Funds

Ticker	Fund Name	Institution
FBIDX	Spartan U.S. Bond Index Fund	Fidelity
FSCLX	Spartan Mid-Cap Index Fund	Fidelity
FSIIX	Spartan International Index Fund	Fidelity
FSSPX	Spartan Small-Cap Index Fund	Fidelity
FUSEX	Spartan 500 Index Fund	Fidelity
NAESX	Vanguard Small Capitalization Index Fund	Vanguard
PESPX	Dreyfus MidCap Index	Schwab
SFLNX	Schwab Fundamental US Large Company Index Fund	Schwab/E*TRADE
SWBDX	Schwab Short-Term Bond Market	Schwab
SWISX	Schwab International Index	Schwab
SWLBX	Schwab Total Bond Market	Schwab
SWPPX	Schwab S&P 500 Index	Schwab
SWSSX	Schwab Small Cap Index	Schwab
VFICX	Vanguard Intermediate-Term Investment-Grade Fund	Vanguard
VFSTX	Vanguard Short-Term Investment-Grade Fund	Vanguard
VGTSX	Vanguard Total International Stock Index Fund	Vanguard
VIGRX	Vanguard Growth Index Fund	Vanguard
VIMSX	Vanguard Mid-Cap Index Fund	Vanguard
VISGX	Vanguard Small Capitalization Growth Index Fund	Vanguard
VISVX	Vanguard Small Capitalization Value Index Fund	Vanguard
VIVAX	Vanguard Value Index Fund	Vanguard
VLACX	Vanguard Large Cap Index Fund	Vanguard
VMGRX	Vanguard Mid-Cap Growth Fund	Vanguard
VMVIX	Vanguard Mid-Cap Value Index Fund	Vanguard
VWESX	Vanguard Long-Term Investment-Grade Fund	Vanguard

Figure B-6: Other Transacton Fee Free Index Funds

Ticker	Fund Name	Institution
DBIRX	Dreyfus Bond Market Index Basic	E*TRADE
DISSX	Dreyfus Small Cap Stock Index Fund	E*TRADE
FLBIX	Spartan Long-Term Treasury Bond Index Fund	Fidelity
FNCMX	Fidelity® NASDAQ Composite Index® Fund	Fidelity
FSBIX	Spartan Short-Term Treasury Bond Index Fund	Fidelity
NOINX	Northern International Equity Index Fund	E*TRADE
NOMIX	Northern Mid Cap Index Fund	E*TRADE
NOSIX	Northern Stock Index Fund	E*TRADE
NSIDX	Northern Small Cap Index Fund	E*TRADE
SVSPX	SSgA S&P 500 Index N	TD Ameritrade
TRCVX	TIAA-CREF Large-Cap Value Idx Retire	TD Ameritrade
TRIEX	TIAA-CREF International Equity Index Fund	TD Ameritrade
TRIRX	TIAA-CREF Large-Cap Gr Idx Retire	TD Ameritrade
TRIRX	TIAA-CREF Large-Cap Gr Idx Retire	TD Ameritrade

Figure B-7: Broad Index Exchange Traded Funds

Ticker	Fund Name	Institution
AGG	iShares Barclays Aggregate Bond	Fidelity
BND	Vanguard Total Bond Market ETF	Vanguard / TD Ameritrade
IJH	iShares Core S&P Mid-Cap ETF	Fidelity
IJR	iShares Core S&P Small-Cap ETF	Fidelity
IVV	iShares Core S&P 500 ETF	TD Ameritrade
IVV	iShares Core S&P 500	Fidelity
IXUS	iShares Core MSCI Total International Stock	Fidelity
SCHA	Schwab U.S. Small-Cap ETF	Schwab
SCHF	Schwab International Equity ETF	Schwab
SCHM	Schwab U.S. Mid-Cap ETF	Schwab
SCHX	Schwab U.S. Large-Cap ETF	Schwab
SCHZ	Schwab U.S. Aggregate Bond ETF	Schwab
VB	Vanguard Small Cap ETF	Vanguard / TD Ameritrade
VEU	Vanguard FTSE All-World ex-US ETF	Vanguard
VO	Vanguard Mid-Cap ETF	Vanguard / TD Ameritrade
VV	Vanguard Large-Cap ETF	Vanguard

Figure B-8: Other Index Exchange Traded Funds

Ticker	Fund Name	Institution
BIV	Vanguard Intermediate-Term Bond ETF	Vanguard / TD Ameritrade
BLV	Vanguard Long-Term Bond Index ETF	Vanguard / TD Ameritrade
BSV	Vanguard Short-Term Bond ETF	Vanguard / TD Ameritrade
IJJ	iShares S&P Mid-Cap 400 Value Index	Fidelity
IJK	iShares S&P Mid-Cap 400 Growth Index	Fidelity
IJS	iShares S&P SmallCap 600 Value Index	Fidelity
IJT	iShares S&P Small-Cap 600 Growth	Fidelity
ILTB	iShares Core Long-Term U.S. Bond	Fidelity
ISTB	iShares Core Short-Term U.S. Bond	Fidelity
IVE	iShares S&P 500 Value Index	Fidelity
IWB	iShares Russell 1000 Index	Fidelity
IWD	iShares Russell 1000 Value Index	Fidelity
IWF	iShares Russell 1000 Growth Index	Fidelity
MDYG	SPDR® S&P 400 Mid Cap Growth ETF	Schwab
MDYV	SPDR® S&P 400 Mid Cap Value ETF	Schwab
SCHG	Schwab U.S. Large-Cap Growth ETF	Schwab
SCHO	Schwab Short-Term U.S. Treasury ETF	Schwab
SCHV	Schwab U.S. Large-Cap Value ETF	Schwab
SLYG	SPDR® S&P 600 Small Cap Growth ETF	Schwab
SLYV	SPDR® S&P 600 Small Cap Value ETF	Schwab
TLO	SPDR® Barclays Long Term Treasury ETF	Schwab
VBK	Vanguard Small Cap Growth ETF	Vanguard / TD Ameritrade
VBR	Vanguard Small Cap Value ETF	Vanguard / TD Ameritrade
VEA	Vanguard FTSE Developed Markets ETF	Vanguard / TD Ameritrade
VOE	Vanguard Mid-Cap Value ETF	Vanguard / TD Ameritrade
VOT	Vanguard Mid-Cap Growth ETF	Vanguard / TD Ameritrade
VTV	Vanguard Value ETF	Vanguard / TD Ameritrade
VUG	Vanguard Growth ETF	Vanguard / TD Ameritrade

Appendix C: Asset Allocation Historical Returns

Figure C-1: Conservatve Allocation Returns

	Cash	All Bonds	90% Bonds 10% Stocks	80% Bonds 20% Stocks
Average Annual Return 2008-2017	0.40%	5.13%	5.68%	6.20%
Best and Worst Annualized Rate of Return between 1968 and 2017				
Best Year	14.04%	30.87%	29.83%	28.78%
Worst Year	0.05%	-4.38%	-3.81%	-4.30%
Best 5 Years	10.93%	19.22%	19.27%	19.32%
Worst 5 Years	0.08%	0.67%	1.16%	1.65%
Best 10 Years	9.04%	14.25%	14.60%	14.95%
Worst 10 Years	0.40%	3.65%	3.51%	3.36%
Standard Dev	3.17%	7.12%	6.90%	7.08%

Figure C-2: Moderate Allocation Returns

	70% Bonds 30% Stocks	60% Bonds 40% Stocks	50% Bonds 50% Stocks	40% Bonds 60% Stocks
Average Annual Return 2008-2017	6.66%	7.08%	7.45%	7.77%
Best and Worst Annualized Rate of Return between 1968 and 2017				
Best Year	27.74%	27.29%	28.94%	30.59%
Worst Year	-7.00%	-9.70%	-12.54%	-17.34%
Best 5 Years	19.37%	19.40%	19.43%	20.17%
Worst 5 Years	2.11%	2.56%	2.52%	1.61%
Best 10 Years	15.28%	15.61%	15.93%	16.24%
Worst 10 Years	3.18%	2.98%	2.76%	2.51%
Standard Dev	7.62%	8.47%	9.53%	10.74%

Figure C-3: Aggressive Allocation Returns

	30% Bonds 70% Stocks	20% Bonds 80% Stocks	10% Bonds 90% Stocks	All Stocks
Average Annual Return 2008-2017	8.03%	8.23%	8.36%	8.42%
Best and Worst Annualized Rate of Return between 1968 and 2017				
Best Year	32.25%	33.90%	35.55%	37.20%
Worst Year	-22.14%	-26.95%	-31.75%	-36.55%
Best 5 Years	22.20%	24.23%	26.26%	28.30%
Worst 5 Years	0.68%	-0.27%	-1.25%	-2.32%
Best 10 Years	16.55%	17.30%	18.18%	19.05%
Worst 10 Years	1.67%	0.73%	-0.28%	-1.36%
Standard Dev	12.06%	13.89%	14.92%	16.41%

Data sources:
Cash–3-month Treasury Bill, Stocks–Standard & Poor's 500, Bonds–Equal parts (25% each) Federal Reserve figures for Moody's Aaa bonds, Moody's Baa bonds, 5-year U.S. Treasury constant maturities, and 10-year U.S. Treasury constant maturities

Appendix D: List of Figures

About the Author

Art Ernst has been analyzing financial products for almost four decades. He has been writing about them for about three decades.

Art earned his M.B.A. at the Wharton Graduate School of Business in 1984 and was the 1981 recipient of the Eugene E. Agger Memorial Award as the top economics graduate at Rutgers College. He began his career on Wall Street directing projects involved with every phase of development of financial products including funds, annuities, loans and retirement plans. Since 1984 he has managed portfolios for individuals and institutions including mutual funds, insurance companies and foundations.

When Art's children were young he formed an independent consultancy to manage affairs in a family-friendly manner. During this period, he shopped for financial services as a regular consumer. This new perspective changed everything. He resolved to address the sales gimmicks, excessive fees, imprudence, and scams he encountered as a 'retail' financial customer.

Additional to his service on behalf of investment management and financial planning clients, Art has written educational pieces to help the public at large avoid common wealth-harming Wall Street tactics. His articles have been published in several journals, magazines and newspapers. He authored "The Final Rip-Off: Reverse Mortgages" and another volume which served as the basis for this guide.

A Registered Investment Advisor first licensed in 1982, Art is a portfolio manager and the Chief Operating Officer at Byrne Asset Management LLC in Princeton, New Jersey.

www.ingramcontent.com/pod-product-compliance
Lightning Source LLC
Chambersburg PA
CBHW051412200326
41520CB00023B/7203